GUARDIAN
OF
WATER

Ayden melton

Contents

CHAPTER ONE THE SLAFT

To the Custos of the Holy Land, Custody of the Holy Land,
Convent of St. Saviour, Jerusalem.

From Ayden melton,
Studium Biblicum Franciscanum, Convent of the Flagellation,
Via Dolorosa, 2nd Station, Jerusalem.

Reverend Father, I take the liberty of writing to you because what you have been told about the slap with which I blessed a Cousin of the Wall at Allenby Bridge is not entirely accurate. As the Reverend Father well knows, an action often has multiple meanings. It is the angle of view that gives it meaning and determines it.

I therefore ask the Reverend Father, our highest authority, guide and Guardian of us Franciscans of the Holy Land, that in formulating your judgment you evaluate the inspiring thought of my act and recall what he himself wisely explained to me once, as in his life there are occasions in which chance is identified with providence.

Wasn't it the case, many years ago, behind my meeting in the refectory of the convent of Assisi with a friar who came from Jerusalem and to whom I spoke throughout lunch of my love for Christian archeology? And wasn't chance identified with providence when the confrere asked me if I wanted to go to Jerusalem to study with him? It was Luca, Reverend Father, our most illustrious archaeologist whose works I knew by heart.

And this time too it was chance and providence that broke into my life regulated by prayer, teaching, excavations, conferences.

I was in my study at the Flagellation. As the Reverend Father will recall, since my bedroom was by now swollen with books and archaeological finds, I asked your permission, which you promptly granted, to occupy a second room on the same corridor communicating with the first. I have installed a coffee burner and I would like the Reverend Father to come and drink it from me one day. Generous friends send me a quality blend from Italy.

In the studio I collected my papers, the photographs of the excavations and the mosaics, all cataloged in order, first the materials from Mount Nebo, then those from Madaba, then those from Umm-er-Rasas. I also keep the coin collection there. It is too precious to leave it in the museum which, as the Reverend Father is well aware, has an entrance in the courtyard of the Flagellation where pilgrims from every country arrive every day. I fear that some of them may be tempted to take away a few coins as a souvenir, causing us irreparable damage.

I am a Franciscan, Reverend Father, but the vow of humility and poverty does not oblige me to keep watch over that treasure of ours. If the Reverend Father had granted my request to equip the museum with a modern security system, the coins would be on display. I insist again, with due respect, on the request. There are some on the market at a good price, I would even settle for a used system. I believe that if the Reverend Father decides to grant it to me, the good name of the Custody would benefit.

Also because the coin collection of the Decapolis and the Arab Province is unique in the world.

So I was in the Coin Studio, as I call it, and I was polishing a piece of gold minted during the reign of

Titus, when someone knocked on the door. I hurriedly put Tito in the box "reserved" for the second century, locked it and placed it next to the last arrival. The architect Massolini, one of our benefactors, at my suggestion had bought from a Bedouin sheikh of Wadi-Rum, to then give us as a gift, an old cardboard box which contained more than a hundred pieces. He had spent a thousand dollars. Among the coins there were at least three that were worth that amount. It was one of those three I was polishing. Reverend Father, I'll be happy to show them to you when you come for that coffee.

Arranged the box behind some voluminous Bibles in the bookcase opposite the desk, among the shekels of the first Jewish anti-Roman revolt - I discovered them at Dominus Flevit under a tile in the floor - and the bronze coins of the second revolt found in a now dry fountain of the Herodion, I opened the door. Rifaat, our man of the day, informed me that there was a Cousin of the Wall in the courtyard who wanted to speak to me.

I reminded him that only pilgrims were allowed into the courtyard of the Flagellation. He spread his arms in desperation and I guessed that the Cousin of the Wall's manner had been as arrogant as it often was. I smiled at the innocent Rifaat.

I got out and saw a tall young man, with short hair, an athletic build, clearly a soldier. He said he had a message for me. He remained silent, as if he were waiting for a nod. I did, and then he spoke rapidly, almost repeating a sentence he had learned by heart. Someone had to meet me for an urgent matter.

You, Reverend Father, are well aware that these are the methods of certain Israeli offices. They call you and don't tell you why. It had already happened to me twice: the first time when I had to provide information on an excavation in Nazareth that didn't even fall under my responsibility, the second time when they asked me about the provenance of a head from the late Roman period that I had lent – the occasion it was an exhibit in Tel Aviv – to a Middle Eastern archeology lecturer. The questions had been very general, but they responded to the Cousins of the Wall's belief that everyone was plotting behind their backs. So recently, when the usual government office summoned me in writing, I didn't show up. And nothing bad happened to me. This time I decided to accept the soldier's invitation.

There was a black car parked at Sant'Anna. The soldier invited me to sit next to him. The car left the Porta di Santo Stefano, went right, the soldier drove fast and safe. He skirted the walls of the Old City, passed the Jaffa Gate, arrived at Zarfat Square and from there took Agron Street. He stopped in front of number 28. On the door I read on a slightly worn brass plaque: "The Israel Institute for Tal-mudic Publications".

As the soldier rang the bell, I got out of the car. The sky was full of low, black clouds moving fast, driven by a cold wind. The door opened, it must have been regulated by an electric device. It overlooked an alley. On the ground some large stones. At the beginning of the alley I saw a tall iron gate, its doors open and fixed to the wall by two large hooks. It was evident that no one had closed them for years. Attached to the gate was a blackened metal plaque with Hebrew inscription:
"Prohibition of posting". I wondered how something could be posted on a gate, but I couldn't find a plausible answer.

The car drove a few yards into the alley, then stopped. I followed her on foot. I realized that there were only three houses and decided that the place reminded those who forgot that life was a kind of dress rehearsal for the afterlife.

I wasn't supposed to be the first to experience that feeling; he could tell from the fact that, of the three houses, two were closed and certainly deserted. Only the third seemed inhabited. On the ground floor I saw an open door. The soldier had meanwhile disappeared. With the pleasure of trespassing on private property into which I had been forced, I entered and walked down a long corridor whose tiled floor was similar to that of the Flagellation. The two buildings were probably built at the same time.

Reverend Father, the corridor, which seemed very long to me, was lined with bookcases. While I focused my attention on a title that I would never have imagined finding in that place, I heard a voice behind me: «Father Matteo, with a coffee I would like to alleviate the sadness that I imagine was caused in you by this temporary contact "with the philosophy of National Socialism and with its prophet, the imaginative Rosenberg».

The voice was serious, gentle, crystal clear but, despite the friendly tone, there was something dark about it. I turned slowly trying to imagine, before seeing it, which face it corresponded to, but I couldn't form an idea.

The man was tall, energetic, wiry. His tanned face made a pleasant contrast to his crew-cut gray hair. The narrow forehead, the aquiline nose, the thin lips gave him a rapacious air. I judged it to be in its sixties and appreciated its elegance. He was wearing perfectly sewn khakis, rubber-soled leather boots, an impeccably pressed blue cotton shirt, he had a subtle perfume on him and it seemed that not an ounce of powder, and the powder there was indeed a lot, the had ever touched.

"I'm pleased to meet you, Father Matteo," he said.

"You're famous around here. I would like one day, when my commitments allow me, to come and visit her famous museum. »

"I hope it happens soon," I replied with deliberate coolness. The man noticed.

"Forgive me if I haven't introduced myself yet. My name is Saul Bialik and I run the Institute. Here are books of high scientific value that might interest you. For a biblical scholar like you, I am sure it would be very pleasant to spend a few hours as our guest."

There was something vaguely menacing about the invitation. I decided to be on guard. I replied that I thanked him, and as soon as I too had found a free moment I would accept the offer. She looked at me carefully. Her gaze was clear.

"I admire her. The Moses Memorial at Mount Nebo is an archaeological treasure, you have uncovered some of the most significant mosaics in the Middle East, and the excavations at Umm-er-Rasas are of high historical and scientific value."

I didn't spare him the joke: «In Umm-er-Rasas more than a thousand years ago people and religions lived together peacefully and today they wage war».

"Yeah," he coughed.

I smiled at him, it was the best I could do. She considered it a sign of a thaw: «Follow me, Father Matteo, I promised you a coffee».

We passed through other corridors filled with books. Saul Bialik named a title, an author, Saint Augustine, Tommaso Campanella, Cervantes, Bernanos, Claudel. I knew it was a bait thrown to create a better climate, but I wanted to taste it anyway.

"It's not about Jewish culture!" I exclaimed in mock astonishment.

"Indeed," he replied satisfied, "there's everything

here. I'd like you to choose a few books.'
"A gift?"

He realized that he had fallen into a trap. He didn't want to contradict himself, but he couldn't even give me a piece of the library. He changed his tone.
"Come on, we'll think about the books later."

Bialik's office was large. In front of the desk I saw some armchairs and on the right I noticed a water dispenser. The floor was covered with a coconut fiber mat. A soft light filtered through the screened windows. The walls were bare, except for one on which was a map of the Old City divided into four areas, marked with a different color, green for Muslim, white for Christian, red for Armenian, yellow for Jewish.

"On June 6, 1967," Bialik said confidingly, "about the forty-eighth hour of the Six Day War, Uzi Narkis, the head of Tsahal, our army, urged Moshe Dayan to enter the Old City . And Moshe replied: "It is excluded, what is the use of all that Vatican?". But a few hours later our government decided to contradict Dayan. Who do you think was right, Moshe or the government?"

I looked at him amazed and didn't answer. She had told me a story that everyone in Jerusalem knew. He continued: "When Tsomet, the section of the Mossad that deals with Arab countries, was born, I was enlisted as an agent. Today I am the deputy director. But I assure you the Institute is not a front. I'm directing it for real. This is the magic of Jerusalem. Moshe Dayan didn't get it. The Old City is not a large Vatican, but the place of our faith and our memory of which Tsomet and the Talmud are two necessary, specular and indivisible moments».
"You understand that I cannot agree."

"When I arrived in Jerusalem many years ago, this was the land of utopia and dreams. We had a homeland, we turned sand into fruit, we discovered water in the deserts, our army was young, thought it was invincible and fought with the heart. Then something happened. And today in the army there are many boys who commit suicide. It happens everywhere, but it's the first time with us. And it's the first time we've had a water problem: Kinneret's reserves, which you call the Sea of Galilee, have greatly diminished. In the future we will have to change our economy and cut agriculture. The Palestinians claim that we violate the Oslo accords and purposely thirst for them. They forget that we are the persecuted ones. History proves it without a doubt." As Bialik spoke, I thought of a ceremony to which I had recently been invited. It was a meeting between Israeli army officers and Holocaust survivors, organized in a Jerusalem theater by a pacifist association. Several elderly people, including twin brothers, had taken their seats on the stage. When their turn came, one of them stood up and said that as children they lived in Vilna, occupied by the Nazis. One day, while they were playing soccer as always with their Christian friends, they were captured and locked up in a train that was to take them to Dachau. The tracks passed next to the soccer field. Through the cracks in the carriage they saw the Christian friends who continued to play. Some officers burst into tears, others left the room visibly moved. In particular, one of them struck me, thin, curly and very young. He impressed me the way he banged his forehead against his rifle. Rhythmically, with an ancient desperation. I thought that Bialik must be suffering like him and that he came from a past similar to that of the twins. He kept talking to me passionately.

"Over a quarter of the Jewish inhabitants of

Jerusalem consider it blasphemous, and therefore do not recognize, the state of Israel. The anti-nationalist Haredim are ultra-Orthodox who wait for the Messiah and dream of the past. The neighborhoods where they live follow the rules of a post-war Central European ghetto.

I asked him if he had ever tried to reflect on the social and spiritual closure of those Sephardic slums inhabited by Iraqi, Moroccan, Tunisian, Yemeni, Ethiopian Jews. He replied that he knew well how their rabbis used to resort to Kabbalah with rites reminiscent of those of the magicians and healers of the ancient Orient. In reality, he would have liked it if in these parts the experience of the shtetl next to Wadi-Rum could be repeated. Approximately five thousand people lived in the shtetl and over the centuries there had been a unique experience, the coexistence of two poor societies, that of the Orthodox Jews and that of the peasants.

"The shtetl, Father Matteo," his tone was passionate now, "didn't represent perfection, but it was a coherent social model."

I shook my head unconvinced. And since, I replied, Jerusalem was the only city in the world sacred to multiple religions and even to opposing groups within the same faith, I found it very difficult from a practical point of view to guarantee full protection for everyone's rights.

"The situation deteriorates when religious feelings are confused with political demands," Bialik said gravely. «The inevitable result is the birth of extremism. The only solution would be for this land of mine to be taken away from God to be returned to men."

He sighed for a long time. And she spoke then in an inspired tone.

"Do you know how I imagine the first Jew to set foot

in the promised land? He has the features of the mythical sabra, the face of a beautiful golden boy. I see the young idealist suffer in the intrigues of politics and the temptation of money. But I know that he hardens himself in battles and in blood. That golden boy is our present, but also our future. Ayden melton, we have been denied access to the Temple Mount where Muslims have built their mosques. What has been destroyed, the Messiah will rebuild."

"Isn't that a form of extremism too?" I asked. He didn't reply, also because at that moment a soldier entered the study with a yellow folder under his arm. Bialik took the briefcase and placed it in front of him on the desk, then quickly gave some instructions to the soldier who clicked his heels and went out.

Saul Bialik opened the briefcase, took out the contents – it could have been a police report – and as he read, an expression of anger, then satisfaction appeared on his face. Watching his long fingers turn the pages, I assumed they were capable of torturing prisoners. And this was enough for me to review the favorable judgment which in the meantime I had formulated regarding him and in which mistrust had mixed with sympathy.

"I was wondering," he interrupted his reading, pulling me from my thoughts, "if you're interested in real, flesh-and-blood killers."
"Maybe yes," I said slowly. "I think yes." Saul Bialik pursed his lips.

«If reality is at the origin of every story, it is often dispersed in incoherent variations, and suddenly suspends the action, leaving the plot and its legitimate conclusion in mid-air. That same reality is also capable of moving away from an interesting path to stubbornly focus on a detail that takes away from the dramatic effects.»

I asked him if he meant the pages he was reading. He nodded to me exclaiming with a certain rhetoric: «Father Matteo, in these papers there is the reality of a murderer!»,

I - but this Bialik could not have known it - was a good reader of detective novels. I was passionate about plots, especially those of Agatha Christie. I found Appointment with Death, his play partly set in Petra, absolutely perfect, perhaps because there were many references to my profession as an archaeologist. I explained to Bialik that I thought a murderer in a crime novel was more humane than a real murderer. In a crime novel there is the victim, the usual suspects, the detective. All of this is artistic. While a real killer has nothing artistic.

Bialik looked at me in amazement. He was amazed at such competence in events so distant from the experience of a priest. I replied that the sacrament of confession allows us to understand many aspects of the human soul. He pointed to the cards in front of him.

"In there is the life of a vulgar and vile individual. Murderer, spy, drug dealer, not counting at least ten bombings."

"The last activity sounds like a certain amount of courage, don't you think?" Saul Bialik replied firmly: "Ayden melton, Khafre never participated in the physical execution of the crimes."

I observed that a terrorist, who assumes that of a pyramid as his stage name, should possess a certain culture. Bialik explained to me that culture had nothing to do with it. The name could suggest a red herring. Tsomet was looking for him in Egypt, because he believed that there he had his origins, refuge and operational base, instead he was Syrian or Lebanese or

Jordanian or even born in Jerusalem. Professionals like him, Bialik added with a certain contempt in his voice, are careful not to risk their lives. They are the link between politicians who have a goal and turn a blind eye to the means to get there, and idealists who are ready to die for their dream. What matters in an attack is not finding out who pulled the trigger, but who paid for the weapon. Only the Khafres can tell about it. And if you catch them, they immediately offer you full availability. They don't like prison and its inconveniences, like harsh interrogation, for example, he concluded in a satisfied tone. I asked him what hard interrogation consisted of. He replied that it was not a pleasant thing to suffer or to look at, but it was inevitable with people of that type. He smiled menacingly and continued contemptuously: 'Courage is not a commodity for sale. Tsahal is at the forefront. Our boys are more and more prepared and the weapons more and more refined. Those who think that our army has changed, that it has collapsed are wrong. Politically we have chosen the path of peace, but the boys of Tsahal can resist any violence, because they have an objective and an ideal, the security of Israel". like a harsh interrogation, for example, he concluded in a satisfied tone. I asked him what hard interrogation consisted of. He replied that it was not a pleasant thing to suffer or to look at, but it was inevitable with people of that type. He smiled menacingly and continued contemptuously: 'Courage is not a commodity for sale. Tsahal is at the forefront. Our boys are more and more prepared and the weapons more and more refined. Those who think that our army has changed, that it has collapsed are wrong. Politically we have chosen the path of peace, but the boys of Tsahal can resist any violence, because they have an objective and an ideal, the security of Israel". like a harsh interrogation, for example, he concluded in a satisfied tone. I asked him what hard interrogation consisted of. He replied that it was not a pleasant thing to suffer or to look at, but it was inevitable with people of that type. He smiled menacingly and continued contemptuously: 'Courage is not a commodity for sale. Tsahal is at the forefront. Our boys are more and more prepared and the weapons more and more refined. Those who think that our army has changed, that it has collapsed are wrong. Politically we have chosen the path of peace, but the boys of Tsahal can resist any violence, because they have an objective and an ideal, the security of Israel". He replied that it was not a pleasant thing to suffer or to look at, but it was inevitable with people of that type. He smiled menacingly and continued contemptuously: 'Courage is not a commodity for sale. Tsahal is at the forefront. Our boys are more and more prepared and the weapons more and more refined. Those who think that our army has changed, that it has collapsed are wrong. Politically we have chosen the path of peace, but the boys of Tsahal can resist any violence, because they have an objective and an ideal, the security of Israel". He replied that it was not a pleasant thing to suffer or to look at, but it was inevitable with people of that type. He smiled menacingly and continued contemptuously: 'Courage is not a commodity for sale. Tsahal is at the forefront. Our boys are more and more prepared and the weapons more and more refined. Those who think that our army has changed, that it has collapsed are wrong. Politically we have chosen the path of peace, but the boys of Tsahal can resist any violence, because they have an objective and an ideal, the security of Israel". Those who think that our army has changed, that it has collapsed are wrong. Politically we have chosen the path of peace, but the boys of Tsahal can resist any violence, because they have an objective and an ideal, the security of Israel". Those who think that our army has changed, that it has collapsed are wrong. Politically we have chosen the path of peace, but the boys of Tsahal can resist any violence, because they have an objective and an ideal, the security of Israel".

It was then that I felt I needed to quote a Bible verse.

"Do not oppress the stranger, for you were strangers in the land of Egypt."

Bialik stood up, shook his head gritting his teeth, I thought he was going to attack me. Then anger turned to satisfaction at the answer he was preparing to give me. He declaimed: "Stupid is the person who believes in his neighbor. Justice exists only for the one whose fists and stubbornness enabled him to claim it."

It was I who stood up in indignation. I almost yelled, "Mr. Bialik, I find it offensive to answer the Bible with a phrase from Iabotinsky. Do you think I don't know who Leev Iabotinsky was? A Jewish fascist, an imitator of Mussolini and Hitler, the founder of Betaa, the brown-shirted paramilitary squads educated in discipline and leader worship. Are you an admirer of Betaa?'

Bialik used a conciliatory tone and reminded me that Iabotinsky considered Italy his spiritual homeland, and defined himself as a disciple of Garibaldi and Mazzini. I interrupted him by quoting from his memory a passage from his letter to Mussolini of 1922: «If you want to know the degree of vitality of the Jews, study your fascists, and add a little more tragedy».

Bialik in a vibrant voice asked me if I knew what the last fighter of the Warsaw ghetto had cried out to God before he died and, without waiting for my answer, he declaimed: "I will always respect your law, but I will not kiss the rod of anyone strikes".

"There is no place for Job in his Israel, is there, Bialik?"
"Please, Father Matteo, leave my thoughts in peace."

I lowered my head, perhaps I had exaggerated. He made a curious gesture. He put his right hand on his neck, pinched it as if to crush an invisible animal, with his own hand he stroked his throat gently for a long time. He sighed, his tone dropping.

"Everyone knows that their requests, however morally founded, are not realistic. It's impossible to make peace with the Arabs, that's what emerges every time I let myself be drawn into a political discussion, on the street, in a cafe. And from some occasional Palestinian interlocutor I hear this reversed argument, it is impossible to make peace with the Jews. When one of us opens our eyes, he knows that one of his compatriots will be injured or killed before dark and that his very existence is at risk. But he doesn't care. At most there are some restrictions. He will not go into shopping malls, he will avoid the streets where attacks have taken place, he will not go to crowded places. He realizes that the cities are increasingly empty, and that sometimes there are more policemen around than passersby. But he got used to that too. The evening, after the umpteenth news report on a funeral in Tel Aviv or Gaza, he murmurs to himself: "Luckily nothing bad happened to me today." Father Matteo, we have only one certainty, even if this word has a somewhat lugubrious sound. We are convinced that, apart from the Palestinians and a few extremists, none of the neighboring Arab states has an interest in provoking a war. The problem is people like Khafre. He understands me?"

I nodded assent. He smiled again and explained that Khafre was just smarter than other terrorists because he had never had his picture taken. The secret services of half of Europe knew of his existence. Also because Chephren was really a great traveller. I told him that he talked about it as if he were dead.

"Yes, he's dead. Last night a fisherman found his body in the Kinneret waters. He had his throat cut and he was floating, from that denial that he was him. If nothing else, he met a violent end. Which already resembles a form of justice."

Saul Bialik's expression changed. He was less harsh now.

"I invited you here for a story that somehow concerns you and has some connection with terrorism."

"You mean with the late Khafre?"

"In a sense." I reacted badly.

"It is nonsense to attribute contacts with terrorists to an archaeologist, a professor of biblical history and geography." Saul Bialik beamed as if I had paid him a compliment. Then he suddenly changed expression. He looked bored.

"Oh yes?"

"Yup."

He laughed heartily as if my yes had a comical flavour. Then she asked me gently: "Do you remember Giulia Lazzari?"

That name caused a strong emotion inside me and made me run back in time. Have you ever thought that, Reverend Father? Memory is our coherence, our reason, our feelings, even our actions. Without it we are nothing. Giulia Lazzari was a piece of my memory. Important, even if short. Because it's not the duration of memories that gives relief, Reverend Father, but their intensity.

Do you remember when I went to Milan to prepare the exhibition on the history of the Custody of the Holy Land at Palazzo Reale? I took the train to Rome. It was mid-April. In the spring, as you know, I teach history and biblical geography at the Gregorian. Giulia Lazzari took a seat in the armchair opposite mine. Her face was regular, the nose small and upturned, the deep blue eyes, the white skin, the shiny, straight, black hair. If I had to give a brief definition of Giulia Lazzari, I would have said that she was fascinating.

Then something bizarre happened. Two drops of sweat appeared symmetrically on either side of her forehead. It seemed to me that they smelled. I couldn't take my eyes off her face. Giulia Lazzari noticed it, she smiled at me.

I think it was fate that gave us those two armchairs. I watched her skin. She was tense now, light, delicate. Express a delicate compliment in this regard. She thanked me and added that her skin had often been the object of admiration. She was the only beautiful thing she wore, she added charmingly, and if I really wanted to, I could even touch her with my fingers. Her voice had many pitches and sudden modulations.
"Are you a priest by any chance?"

I looked at her amazed. I was wearing, as always - and I know you don't like it, even if faith has nothing to do with the habit - a dark gray suit, a blue shirt and black shoes with rubber soles, good for every season .
"How did you figure that out?" I asked her.

"From his eyes and the way he spoke to me. A normal man would have said other words." He realized that the word "normal" could be offensive and added:
«You are perfectly normal, forgive me, I don't want you to misinterpret me. In short, I think you are a good person. I feel".

I would have liked to explain to Giulia Lazzari how priesthood and goodness are often not perfect traveling companions, but perhaps it would have been

inappropriate and probably she would not have understood me. I asked her what her profession was.
"I'm a singer," she replied proudly.

He told me about his father, who had been dead for a few months. He was a tenor, operetta singer. He had wanted her to follow his career. So she had studied with patience, and self-sacrifice, and now at twenty-five she was ready. She asked me what kind of priest I was, I explained to her that I was a friar and a scholar, I directed the Studium Biblicum Franciscanum museum in Jerusalem and the Franciscan archaeological mission of Mount Nebo, where the biblical tradition claimed that Moses was buried. And there, many years before, the faithful had built a church which was called precisely Memorial of Moses. I had helped restore it and had found some of the most beautiful mosaics in the Middle East.

I told her how the road to get up there went through barren places and stony hills. He asked me what the colors of spring and summer were at the Nebo. I replied that, unlike many other places, the colors were always the same at Nebo. Time in the stones had stopped, perhaps to remember Our Lord's earthly passage. I told her about when, walking in the desert, in front of my feet I saw something that looked like a stone, but it was too smooth to be really. A few steps later I saw others, identical to the first. I took one in my hands and realized that I was holding a razor-sharp axe, ready for hunting, thousands upon thousands of years old. I counted more than thirty. I had come across a cemetery of prehistoric axes, one more perfect than the other.

Giulia Lazzari looked at me in astonishment, then told me that my passion for that land moved her. I explained to her that that land also included Jerusalem and I told her that I loved every stone of the Holy Land

and wanted to explore them all.

Giulia Lazzari told me about her voice, the difficulties of her artistic career and her father's sacrifices. He was Italian and his mother Lebanese Maronite Christian. She was born in Beirut. She had lost her parents in an accident. Their car had hit a mine. She didn't know if the mine was Maronite, Druze, Syrian, Israeli. She now she was going to Milan where she had an audition. They were looking for the protagonist of the Merry Widow for the Trieste Operetta Festival.

Saul Bialik was staring at me, perhaps to understand my thoughts. He said he had a surprise for me. Giulia Lazzari was his guest and had asked to meet me. I asked him which hotel he was staying in. Bialik laughed heartily.

«In a very safe hotel, Father Matteo. And he's waiting for her."

Outside his office the usual soldier told me to follow him. My surprise was great when, instead of leaving the building, the soldier accompanied me to the basement. There was humidity and a bad smell. A long spiral staircase, a dark and damp corridor, some cells. He opened one and I saw Giulia Lazzari, who came towards me and embraced me passionately. She whispered to me, "Thank you."

"How did the audition go?"

"Very well," she smiled at me, "I've been signed. At the first I had eight calls. My Countess excited and moved the audience. How many flowers have I received, and Pascal's roses were the reddest. I got drunk on success, perfume and love that night." I asked her who Pascal was.

«You're right, when we met, Pascal Aretz didn't exist yet. First I met his roses, then he appeared in the dressing room and I fell in love in an instant and forever. How do you become friends in an instant and forever, right, Father Matteo?»

Tears flooded her face. Between her sobs he uttered words of love in Italian and French. She squeezed my hands confidently.

"Pascal is the only man who has been good to me. Life is not very happy for a single woman pursuing a certain career. Do you understand me?"

I said yes and said I was happy for her. But I didn't understand why she was in a dank cell, treated like a prisoner. Giulia Lazzari sighed for a long time. She said: «At first I didn't know who Pascal was, it didn't matter. We went to Paris, a passionate love ours, as happens in an opera. But it was real. After a few days he told me that he was of the Melkite religion, fled from his home Palestine because the Israelis persecuted him. He worked for peace, but they didn't understand. I lived with Pascal between Paris and Amman, without giving up on his career. Lately I sang in Munich, in Berlin, in Vienna and finally in Paris. From Paris I had decided to return to Amman via Jerusalem to visit those stones that she loves so much. At the Ben Gurion passport control they stopped me and after a long wait two men brought me here without an explanation. Then a mean-looking gentleman asked me questions about Pascal. I remembered her and told the gentleman that we are her friends. What I regret is that I have not been able to visit Jerusalem. But I am convinced that she will take me out of this horrible place and show me her dear stones. Will you do it, Father Matteo?"

I promised. Her face had a peculiar expression. Do you know, Reverend Father, when we are about to leave for the holidays and our thoughts are already there? Giulia greeted me with this state of mind. Or so she thought.

Two minutes later I was staring at Saul Bialik's ankles. Socks that were too short left them uncovered. I noticed that tiny blue veins tangled around my ankles, identical to mine. They had always irritated and annoyed me because they represented the first sign of old age. I concluded that Bialik and I were the same age. But it wasn't possible. As the Reverend Father knows, I turned fifty-seven a few days ago. So, I thought with a certain melancholy, I don't wear well my years.

Bialik looked at me smiling, touched his ankles and commented: "There are some veins, youth is gone."

Maybe he didn't realize I had the same problem. But somehow the joke gave him an advantage over me. I suddenly felt old.

"It often happens," Bialik added, as if he understood and wanted to console me, "that those veins appear at a certain age. Is not serious."

"Yeah," I replied curtly.

"How is Giulia Lazzari?"

He was in a damp cell, I protested, and I didn't understand the reason for that cruelty towards an innocent woman.

"Pascal Aretz!" Saul Bialik exclaimed. "Isn't that reason enough?" He continued:

«Pascal Aretz, born in Nazareth, studied Arabic Language and Literature at the Sorbonne and, after having taught in some French universities, he settled in Paris. He belongs to a wealthy Melkite family. Three years ago he returned to Nazareth. In Paris he directed a monthly review of Arab studies and collaborated on a regular basis with some newspapers, in short, he enjoyed 'a good position. For this reason its return made us suspicious. He was later seen in Emmaus, Jericho, Gaza, Ramallah, Nablus and finally settled in Bethlehem in the Melkite seminary of Beit Sahur. Then he disappeared. From that moment we convinced ourselves, even without having proof, that he was a terrorist. Recently he was living in Amman with an operetta singer, Giulia Lazzari.'

"Then?" I asked.

"I want to hear from you."

"I really don't know what to tell her. Often in your war it is very easy to call an idealist a terrorist."

"In this war, terrorists and idealists often identify with each other and we cannot afford confusion or weakness. We need to talk to Pascal Aretz, because, after Chephren's death, he could be the new leader of that band of assassins."

"Just talk?"

"To talk, to question. It's the same thing."

I observed that was his point of view. Because some interrogations start one way and end another. She exclaimed with a touch of annoyance that they were subtleties and I retorted that the life of a human being wasn't quite a subtlety.

"You can convince Giulia Lazzari to arrange for Pascal Aretz to come this side of the Jordan. It's your friend's only chance to save herself from being accused of espionage."

"Bialik, don't be ridiculous. Giulia Lazzari doesn't even know what the word spy means."

«But we do. I need to talk to Pascal Aretz. I have a card in my hand and I play it."

I asked him with a touch of astonishment if he really thought I could convince Giulia Lazzari to betray her man. He smiled, shrugged, shook his head and said with the tone of one who makes a precious confidence: "In our work we try, we try, in the end we get some results, thanks also to the help of disinterested friends like you".

I overlooked his irony. Now she was almost begging me. "Convince her."

I asked what the guarantees were. He frowned and said someone had referred to him as a skilled negotiator. I asked him who that person was.

"I'm not authorized to reveal it," he said almost officially. I stiffened. Bialik noticed. His voice was grave.

«Which side are you on, Father Matteo?» I replied that a priest prays for everyone.

"For me too?"

"Of course."

He recited: "Cynism is the highest that can be achieved on earth. To conquer it you need the strongest fists and the most delicate fingers».

I stared at him coldly and told him I'd be back soon. The following day Giulia Lazzari welcomed me with a big smile.

«They have to let me go free, Father Matteo. They're holding me to spite Pascal. I know, they think he's a terrorist, but Pascal is just a patriot. I want her to visit him in Amman and tell him I'm fine. And I would be grateful if you would give him a letter from me."

He gave me a crumpled sheet.

"You can read, they are words of love."

Giulia Lazzari took my hands in hers and squeezed them affectionately. Her eyes were happy and looked bluer to me. She brought her face close to mine and whispered:

"I'm expecting a baby. Pascal doesn't know it and neither do they."

He pointed to the door with a defiant gesture.

"Pascal was worried because my head was spinning and I fainted. These are things that happen in these circumstances, I would like you to reassure him. Don't tell him I'm pregnant because our son shouldn't cause him any problems. Pascal has a mission to accomplish."

I understood at that moment, Reverend Father, how complicated the situation was. I had to act with circumspection. I went to talk to Saul Bialik who asked me brusquely if I had convinced Giulia Lazzari. In a way, I answered him. Perhaps I had found a way to induce Pascal Aretz to come with me to the Allenby Bridge Police Station. There he would meet with him. After the interview, Pascal Aretz would return to Jordan and Giulia Lazzari would join him in Amman. Bialik reacted sharply: "Impossible, that man is a terrorist."

"There's no evidence," I replied calmly. "She said it, Bialik. And she also explained to me that she just wants to talk to him."

Bialik reluctantly agreed. But Giulia Lazzari would have been released after the meeting.
"Before." I said firmly.

Bialik exclaimed that I was quite a good negotiator and concluded, "Okay. But Giulia Lazzari will start where she came from, from Ben Gurion. Your destination will be a European city.'

Reverend Father, at this point I could consider myself moderately satisfied with the result achieved. So I went to Amman to see Pascal Aretz. The address Giulia had given me corresponded to a neighborhood in the hills, where the best Palestinian society of the diaspora lived, the families who fled Jerusalem in '48. I telephoned to warn of my arrival and a waiter told me that I would find the professor in Cerasa. He would stay all day in the Southern Theater. I would have recognized him easily because he was wearing a black safari jacket and a white cap with a red visor. I had been missing from Cerasa for some time, which I consider, Reverend Father, the most beautiful Roman city in the East. In my opinion it is even more important and harmonious than Ostia Antica. I hope you agree with my assessment.

I recognized Professor Aretz immediately. He was on the stage of the Southern Theater. As if he was waiting for me, he waved me over. He shook my hand silently, with a smile. The squeeze of that large, strong, reassuring hand was not only a conventional and courteous gesture, but the sign of trusting attention. His face was singular, his forehead high and broad, half hidden by a tuft of hair they left a thin, very white line exposed above the arch of the eyebrows. A face which, despite the hardness of the features, the nose slightly enlarged at the tip, the pale and thin lips, appeared very sweet.

Pascal Aretz was no more than thirty-five and certainly nothing about him indicated that he was a terrorist. I don't mean, Reverend Father, that terrorists have something on their faces that makes them recognizable, but nothing ambiguous, elusive, dangerous came to me from Pascal Aretz. I saw in front of me a young scholar with clear and clear manners who said to me: «The theater is in perfect condition. Whenever possible, I come here and calm down».

Then was the spell. A very pure voice with agile high notes and confident harmonies intoned the Gloria of Schubert's Mass No. 5, giving me great joy. In the end I applauded for a long time, moved. Pascal Aretz showed me a small tape recorder.

"I always carry it with me. Don't you think that Giulia should interpret this kind of music and no longer operetta?» I answered yes. She told me that she knew me by reputation, that she was waiting for me. Then he concluded with a smile: «Do you know that we do the same job?».

"Are you a friar?"

"No, an archaeologist," he smiled at me gravely. "I'm about to start an excavation right here."

"Inside the Southern Theater?" I asked amazed.

He didn't answer me. He said instead: "I have a degree in Arabic language and literature and few people know that I have a second degree in archeology". He paused. "Giulia told me a lot about you."

"He's only seen me twice."

"He holds her in high regard. Tell me about her, please."

"He's fine and he loves her."

I was puzzled. Who warned him of my visit? He replied that before leaving Paris, Giulia had told him that she would be staying in Jerusalem for a couple of days to meet me. I replied that since he hadn't warned me, he might as well not have found me. I was often travelling. Pascal Aretz smiled.

«Julia is an optimist.» She changed her tone. He was worried.

"So, how is he?"

"Good. But you didn't answer my question."

"I got a phone call."

"From who?"

"What do the Tsomet people want from me?"

"Speak."

"What if I don't trust you?"

"I'm here, you have to trust me."

I gave him Giulia's letter. He read it over and over and her eyes watered.

«Father Matteo, who do you work for?»

"For peace."

He stared at me ironically.

"Every nation of men shall reside according to their blood in the lands and boundaries established by God."
I asked him what its boundaries were.

«The borders of my land are complicated borders. Our Lord preached charity. Charity is love. Love means giving generously, even sacrificing one's life. We live in a society where there is no justice, there are refugees and prisoners, people forgotten by all who await a better tomorrow. The role of someone like me is to bear witness to God's trust in all men. I am a Melkite by oriental vocation and by love. I assure you that I have not killed or caused anyone to be killed. I live here because they prevent me from living in my land as a free man, and from teaching as a free man. The faithful of the Melkite Church in the Galilee and around Jerusalem are Palestinians. Our problems are the problems of the Arab people. In Galilee our church was very well organized and had many believers. Many of us were forced to leave our villages and found themselves refugees in Lebanon. Those who remained have suffered persecution and are trying to resist. Before, when I was free to travel to Jerusalem, I didn't cross the Allenby or King Hussein bridge, as they call it in these parts. From Amman I flew to Cyprus and from there I flew to Israel. Because that bridge over the Jordan divides the same land in two. And I can't accept it." Because that bridge over the Jordan divides the same land in two. And I can't accept it." Because that bridge over the Jordan divides the same land in two. And I can't accept it."

"Julia is expecting a child." Pascal Aretz shook his head and laughed.

"She's very skilled. Giulia must have made her swear not to tell me anything." I didn't answer him.

"Do the Tsomet people know that?"

"No."

"My life for my son's. Is that so?"

"I vouch for your son, for Giulia and for you too." I heard disbelief and a hint of contempt in her voice.

"Do you also guarantee for me? I want to tell you a story, Father Matteo. Some time ago I found myself having a dinner with some Israelis from a high social class. A university professor, a surgeon, a lawyer. We began to talk about this and that and at a certain point, to revive the conversation which was very boring, I told the story of Petra, rediscovered after many centuries by a Swiss archaeologist. They listened to me with interest and attention. Then one of them, I think the surgeon, turned to the other two saying that they had to visit this Petra and asked me what was the best season to go there. I explained that the summer in those parts was very hot and the winter rather harsh. It was then that the surgeon candidly told me that none of the three of them knew Petra's whereabouts. Because it was an Arab city and the Arab world,

Pascal Aretz cupped his face in his hands, his fingers dug hard into the skin.

"Ayden melton, I know where Petra is."

I went to Mount Nebo that afternoon. I stayed for a long time praying in church. I was hoping to save them. They seemed to me so rich in innocence. In the evening Pascal joined me. We dined on spaghetti with sauce that Garbo, my Syrian handyman –the Reverend Father certainly remembers it, Garbo lives permanently at Nebo where he welcomes pilgrims, looks after the sanctuary and cooks – he had prepared for us.

"These spaghetti are excellent," observed Pascal. "At least I'll be able to tell the Tsomet folks I ate spaghetti they'll never get to taste."

He also drank Garbo's wine. Reverend Father, I sent

you some bottles, but you didn't let me know if you like them. It's strong, the Nebo grapes don't grow and we have to buy them from the orthodox priest in Madaba, who charges us a little too much. If I think about what the Orthodox have done in the restoration of the dome of the Holy Sepulcher I get a fit of bile. We talked a lot about it that evening with Pascal and he too was in complete agreement. Then he told me that Jerusalem had an added value. That's exactly what he said. For the concentration within it of an exceptional number of holy places. He told me that he was thrilled to be with me on the mountain where God had ordered Moses to climb, saying to him: «Go to Mount Nebo which is in the land of Moab, opposite Jericho, and look at the land of Canaan which I am giving to the children of Israel.

I appreciated the quote. As the evening was clear, I showed him the lights of Jericho and the Mount of Olives. He was moved, looked at me affectionately, hugged me and said: «Always remember, Arafat does not want to be remembered as the man who sold off the Esplanade of the Mosques where the Al-Aqsa mosque is located, the third holiest place in the world. 'Islam". And he concluded. «It is my ambition to accomplish something important and decisive. I've often thought I could if I had the time."
It was at that point that he asked me point-blank: "Can I trust you?"

I begged him to listen to me carefully. I offered him another glass of wine and told me that I was born in Ginostra, on the island of Stromboli, a few meters from the sea which was clean, transparent, wild. Around the house there was a vegetable garden, a chicken coop and some fruit trees. Near the garden my mother had planted a mimosa, a rose bush and some flowers. That corner she proudly called our garden. Two cats lived with us, Mustafà and Nenè, brother and sister. My father had them sterilized after a single mating. One afternoon, therefore, I was in "our garden" and I was trying to fix an old rocking chair. I was ten years old and had a natural dexterity in my hands, which later contributed to my success as an archaeologist. I heard something like a long, high-pitched moan. Mustafà appeared and he had a mouse in his mouth. Mustafà's long mustache intertwined with the mouse's tail which beat the air up and down with strength and desperation. Mustafa sank his teeth with cruel slowness into the neck of the mouse which emitted something similar to a sigh. He lasted a long time. When he finished I had the feeling that someone was watching me. I turned around and saw a larger mouse not far from me: he was staring at me motionless. I assumed it was the mother of the little mouse that in the meantime Mustafà had abandoned at my feet. Mother mouse looked at her son and then at Mustafa, now distracted and absent, and disappeared into the grass. in the neck of the mouse which let out something like a sigh. It lasted a long time. When it finished I had the feeling that someone was watching me. I turned around and saw a larger mouse not far from me: it was staring at me motionless. I assumed it was the mother of the little mouse that in the meantime Mustafà had abandoned at my feet. Mother mouse looked at her son and then at Mustafa, now distracted and absent, and disappeared into the grass. in the neck of the mouse which let out something like a sigh. It lasted a long time. When it finished I had the feeling that someone was watching me. I turned around and saw a larger mouse not far from me: it was staring at me motionless. I assumed it was the mother of the little mouse that in the meantime Mustafà had abandoned at my feet. Mother mouse looked at her son and then at

Mustafa, now distracted and absent, and disappeared into the grass.

That evening I dined reluctantly. I was scared and shaken by the violence I had witnessed. I went to bed early. I slept a restless sleep, could not find the position, and when I woke up, I saw mother mouse. She was standing on her half legs of the bed, stared at me. I thought I was dreaming. It was not like this. I made a movement and the mother mouse jumped off. I convinced myself that she had come to communicate her suffering to me. Why had she chosen me?

I spent the morning reading, I was disturbed. After lunch I went back to my room to get some papers. I had to finish a paper for school. On the bed Mustafà was purring. Under one paw, mother mouse was dying. I came closer. Without looking at me, Mustafa blew loudly to tell me that I had to keep my distance. Mother Mouse suffered for a long time. When she finally died, Mustafà stopped purring and remained motionless with his eyes in space.

I think it was precisely that story, the meaningless rape of two mice, that oriented my heart and mind towards the helpless and the weak. A man of God, by contract and by vocation, loves and protects those who suffer. But the death of mother mouse and her son made me smell the suffering, helping me to understand how the life of a humiliated and offended person is very easy to destroy. And the Holy Land, populated by despair and victims, gave me an opportunity that perfected my contract with God.

Pascal Aretz said nothing. He asked me where his room was. I pointed to it. She was close to mine. The next morning, while drinking coffee, he said to me: "Do you guarantee for Giulia and the baby?"

"Yup. They will leave for Paris.'

"Agree. Now I'm ready."

We arrived at the bridge. The Jordanian policemen absentmindedly looked at our documents. On the other side they were waiting for us. Saul Bialik met us with two soldiers. Pascal said to me: "Remember, Father Matteo, what I told you, I know where Petra is."
Then he asked me, "Have you read Peter Pan?"

I looked at him surprised. He recited aloud: "To die, says Peter Pan, will be a terribly great adventure."

Pascal reached into his pocket to take out something that shone in the sun, perhaps a pistol, and started running towards the soldiers. I heard Bialik shout, the soldiers fired. Pascal died without making a sound, without moving an arm or a leg, without contracting a muscle. Only at the last moment, as if in response to a thought, to a whisper that none of us was able to hear, did an ironic look appear on his face that gave his death mask an unusual expression. His gaze, instead of glassy emptiness, communicated absolute satisfaction. I realized that in his hands he was holding a small silver frame with Giulia's photo. I took it from him and swept it across Bialik's face.

Not far from us there was a fat soldier who was eating spaghetti with sauce in a large plate as if nothing had happened. Reverend Father, it was spaghetti that offended me. I felt them as a profanation, an offense to Pascal's last acts of life. I calmly approached, gently took the plate away from the soldier, threw it over his head and concluded my action with a slap. Then I turned to Saul Bialik who was watching me impassively and asked him: "Where's Giulia Lazzari?"

"I assume they're taking you to the airport," she replied.

"So, Bialik, I need your car." He didn't deny it to me. Bialik's driver drove fast. In little more than an hour we were at the Ben Gurion. Giulia had not yet embarked. She asked me: "How is Pascal?"

"Good."

"From Paris I will take a plane to Amman."

"Pascal wants you to stay in Paris." She looked at me in surprise.

"And he prefers she doesn't look for him at this time. She told me she would understand." Giulia nodded thoughtfully.

"He's a great man. Does he love me?"

"Yup. I told him she is expecting a child by him." She threw her arms around my neck.

"I was sure he would tell her. I was sure, but I didn't want to force her, I trusted her sensitivity."

"Pascal wants your child to be born away from here." Julia shook her head.

"Do you remember our train ride? When we said goodbye I wanted to tell you something and I couldn't."

"What did he want to tell me?"

«That his description of the stones excited me. I wanted to assure her that her stones would one day become mine too. If you speak to Pascal before I do, explain to him that our child will be born in this country, among these stones. »

I handed her a crucifix.

"Pascal wants me to carry it with me at all times."

I don't know if Giulia Lazzari understood anything. She pressed him to her heart.

"It's proof that he's okay," I continued.

I waited for Giulia Lazzari to pass passport control and then went back to the car. The driver took me to the

Flagellation. Only then did I realize that it was the same soldier who had come to get me when I first met Bialik. It seemed to me that he was looking at me disapprovingly.

Here, Reverend Father, I think I have told you everything. I realize, however, that as far as the slap is concerned, I've gone too far. Too emotional a reaction. A pastor of souls, even if his patience has been tested, must never get caught up in an impulse so inappropriate to his ministry.
I hope I explained myself and that my reasons are accepted by you. Reverend Father, in the land of Israel whoever does not believe in miracles is not realistic. With my most respectful regards.

Ayden melton.

CHAPTER TWO THE KEEPER

Finding things that belong to you have been touched and looked at by strangers is unpleasant. So when I entered the Coin Office after having sent Rifaat to deliver the letter to the Keeper and I noticed that someone had rummaged through my drawers, the first reaction was anger. Calmer, I tried to think. It was certainly a visitor who would have liked to remain secret. In fact, the books on the floor were intact. But on the desk, where the visitor's attention had stopped, many papers were not in the position in which I had left them. I thought he might be a very inexperienced thief, or someone who had wanted to leave me a warning. Bialik perhaps? What if I got back in time to catch the visitor in the act? I spent half a minute imagining the scene. I thought back to the last few hours. I woke up very early as always. I had dressed, I had gone down to the courtyard. I had delivered the letter to Rifaat. Perhaps Rifaat, on leaving to go to San Salvatore, to the Custos, had left the door of the convent ajar. But Rifaat was very conscientious. Such an oversight seemed impossible to me.

Snow had fallen in Jerusalem that morning. The crisp air and snow made me think that the atmospheric conditions were the same as on the day of Our Lord's birth. But I was not one of the Magi. I had celebrated mass in our chapel built on the stones where, according to medieval tradition, Jesus had been subjected to the torture of the scourge. Therefore it was called the chapel of the Flagellation. At the end of the Mass I had gone to the refectory for breakfast and then to the Study of Coins. In all, I calculated, an hour. In that hour the visitor had been looking for something that I possessed and that interested him.

When I was nervous or worried and had time on my hands, I enjoyed reading a book in the tub filled to the brim with very hot water. I immersed myself with pleasure thinking that fear of the future sometimes conditions our present. I shouldn't have fallen into the trap. If someone meant to spy on me I would find out.

After I got out of the bathroom, I dressed, went to the Coin Studio and checked some 3rd century pieces. I heard a knock on the door. It was Rifaat with the Keeper's answer. I asked him if by chance he had left the convent door open and he absolutely denied it. All that remained was the hypothesis of a brother. An evil thought occurred to me. I could have confessed all the brothers of the Studium and I would have discovered the culprit. But I would have been bound by the bond of the sacrament. And then at that moment at least twenty friars slept at the Flagellation. I read the Keeper's note. He didn't understand why I had written to him, the Studium was no more than a twenty minute walk from San Salvatore. In any case, he was waiting for me at midday mass.

I left the Flagellation, walked along the Via Dolorosa as far as the crossroads with the road that descends from the Damascus Gate, turned left passing in front of the Terza, Fourth, Fifth and Sixth Stations, then right and left again. I walked quickly, I greeted a Melkite Christian Palestinian who was selling rosaries, statuettes and other objects of worship. From the Arab quarter I passed into the Armenian-Christian quarter. I arrived in San Salvatore.

The Custody had moved there in the mid-1500s, when they had expelled us Franciscans from the Last Supper. With the help of the Venetians we had purchased the Convent of the Column from the Georgian monks, the current San Salvatore, where the Custos of the Holy Land resides who has the privilege of episcopal insignia and extends his jurisdiction over the monasteries of Jordan, Israel, the Lebanon, Syria, Cyprus, Lower Egypt and Rhodes.

I went to say hello to Father Vidigal, the librarian. The library, a square room on the ground floor, overlooked an internal courtyard and had only two windows from which, even at noon, little light entered. Vidigal cataloged by hand with amused patience and memorized the title, publisher and location of each book. His head, he said, worked better than any machine. Sure, he could die soon and he felt the need to find someone to replace him. But the young friars seemed to him lazy. He bitterly concluded that his successor would be a computer.

Noon was two minutes past, the Keeper was on his knees in front of the altar. In the private chapel there were only Guillermo, his assistant, Vidigal, who had followed me, and two friars I didn't know. The Keeper turned away, I thought I saw a Sign of disapproval in his eyes. I thought it was the two-minute delay that irritated him. His punctuality was known. He celebrated mass. In his homily he spoke in an inspired tone of Jesus and of his presence in the heart of anyone with the desire to live better. He explained that Jesus sometimes requires sacrifices that may seem risky or unnecessary, but instead fit into a higher vision of the sacred and perfect mystery. He concluded with a complex reasoning. The goal of religion is to make people understand that there is truth first and then force. Men, he cried,

If so, I thought, he'd already acquitted me and we'd never talk about the slap again. With the sensation of being the recipient of his words, I communicated, and the Custos gave me the Sacrament with paternal sympathy. I convinced myself that he had also forgiven my delay. At the end of Mass Guillermo came up to me and told me that the Custos was inviting me to have a frugal meal with him. I couldn't help but observe that the Keeper let me warn at the last moment. Guillermo replied:

"Details".

The frugal meal was prepared in a small room next to the Guardian's study. I found him already seated at the table and I wondered how he had managed to be so fast. I imagined that a secret stairway connected the private chapel with his apartment. It was Guillermo who served us. Tortellini in broth, roast chicken, baked potatoes.

The Guardian said: «I love tortellini in broth very much, but I have some health problems. I can't indulge in certain delicacies. I hope you like them."

He drank some broth. I remarked, "They're excellent."

Perhaps I could have said something less banal. But that was all I could think of. The Keeper looked at me with an air that seemed to me to be affectionate.

"I take it you liked that Pascal Aretz guy."

"He was a man of valor who sacrificed his life to save that of his wife and unborn child."

The Keeper smiled at me.

"I wouldn't get carried away with sentimentality if I were you."

"Why, Reverend Father?"

"Its hero is said to have been the late Khafre's lieutenant."

"Are you also aware of Khafre's death?"

"Maybe we have the same sources. Or maybe not. The news travels to Jerusalem."

"And there's also a rumor that I'd make a good negotiator."

The Keeper smiled without answering me. I said firmly that to me Pascal Aretz hadn't seemed like a terrorist, let alone a murderer.

"Appearances are often deceiving. It's a cliché but it tastes like truth."

I observed that Pascal Aretz used the weapons at his disposal and I could not blame him for that, he had no individual goals, the goal was the freedom of his country.

"From the looks of it, it seems she believes her actions have a justification."

I almost apologized.

"Reverend Father, I have done no wrong in thinking that there was something in him worthy of admiration and respect."

The Keeper looked into my eyes for a long time and, as if talking to himself, said that he had not yet established whether men dedicated to that kind of activity interpreted them with passion or kept their cool. And he added: "Father Matteo, I imagine you know that the most popular sport in Jerusalem is not golf or tennis, but espionage."

I replied that I knew.

"But no one communicates directly with the adversary. It would be simpler, it would avoid many misunderstandings. The confrere from Bologna who gave us the tortellini will return to Italy. He will go to Assisi. He asked for it." I tried to be witty: "But that way we won't eat tortellini anymore!"

«The tortellini can be recovered in some way, but as far as the work of the dear brother is concerned, it is a bit difficult to find a substitute. You taste the chicken for me too. Is it cooked just right?

I replied that it was excellent. The Keeper raised his head and, perhaps referring to something he had recently read, said, 'There is no common sense in this country. A few days ago an Israeli soldier entered the church of Sant'Antonio and shot all the venerated statues of our saints. Before the police intervened, that neo-zealot had managed to fire three rounds from his service machine gun. Perhaps I am thinking too simply when I say that it would not take much to reach an agreement. And instead the agreement seems to be impossible. Israelis enjoy a surround our sanctuaries. In Capernaum, near Peter's house, they have inaugurated a holiday village open to nudists. For what purpose?".

I replied that the purpose seemed obvious to me. He shook his head.

«No, they know very well that they cannot drive us out of Capernaum, much less out of Jerusalem. They are, how to say, small daily difficulties. Maybe random, I don't think the prime minister ordered it, no, it's a question of mentality.

"To remind us of Calvary."

«Yes, Calvary. Two thousand years have flown by. Jesus' journey has continued ever since and will always continue and, even if we are not the strongest religion in the Holy Land, the presence of Our Lord is made more evident not only by the tradition of these places but also by the excavations carried out by archaeologists of value such as she. Archeology completes the philosophical work, the exegesis of the Holy Scriptures, and demonstrates how tradition is an important presupposition of truth. And in the tradition we must also include the tales of pilgrims, with descriptions of their devoted journey.

I thought that the Custos had a strong sense of the presence in the Holy Land and of the authority he represented, but at times he ran the risk of being a bit rhetorical and pedantic. But that too was his charm. He went on to tell me that he had spoken to Shimon Peres after his defeat. That Moshe Katsan, elected president of the republic instead of him, was not well known. It was a clear revenge of the Sephardim and the Orthodox.

"Did you know that some of them, the most extremist, claim that when they enter a cinema they feel like they are inside a gas chamber because they are exposed, in spite of themselves, to the poisonous effects of the films shown?"

The Guardian shook his head and said that Shimon Peres harbored the illusion that Israeli-controlled territory could be divided into two ethnically pure nation states, one Israeli and the other Palestinian. Arafat instead dreamed of wiping the Jewish state off the map, of reducing Jews to a minority in an Arab Palestine.

For the Keeper, the end of the partition utopia was good news. Any negotiation should have started from the idea that in the future Palestine there would be a significant number of Jews, just as there was a significant number of Arabs within Israel. As for its destruction, shouted by some irresponsible people, it was a horror scenario, certainly not immediate. It rested on anti-Israel hatred in the Arab world, as well as on the demographic factor. The return of four million Palestinian refugees, on which Yasser Arafat continued to insist, would have been the premise. In the long run, the Jewish state would be engulfed in that tide. Any kind of peace negotiation would have failed. Only violence would remain. It was clear, for the Keeper, that the myth of total control of Jerusalem was not compatible with the security of Israel. She smiled as if remembering something pleasant.

"Once at sunrise I would take my horse and cross the hills of Samaria alone. From our farm in Turas, in the

Lands of the Patriarchate, to the Arab city of Nablus. To my left I saw the depression falling towards the Dead Sea and to the right the heights full of olive trees that descend to the gates of Jerusalem.

"I didn't know you loved riding like your brother Girolamo."

«Those of Girolamo Mihaic at Mount Nebo were glorious times» sighed the Keeper nostalgically.

He returned to the present. He had met with Rabbi Moshe Hirsh, the head of Neturei Karta. Arafat had promised him the ministry of Jewish affairs in the future Palestinian state. Hirsh was a droll little man with blue eyes in his sixties. He followed his particular reading of the Torah. The state of Israel had no right to exist until the coming of the Messiah, and any Jewish territorial claim was therefore completely absurd and usurpatory against the Arabs. Hirsh's followers paid no taxes, did no military service. In their case, logic and religion got along. He had asked Hirsh how he could accept that Arafat had recognized Israel. Hirsh replied that for Arafat it was a question of safeguarding the things of this world, that is, a piece of land. Instead, he was concerned with something far more precious, the will of God and the Holy Scriptures. The Keeper paused for a long time. He then exclaimed, "An Israeli poet wrote that

Jerusalem is the Venice of God».

'If I may,' I replied, 'that doesn't strike me as a convincing definition. Do you remember, Reverend Father, what Ben Gurion said? Israel will become a state when it has its thieves and prostitutes. If I were the head of government today, I would order a monument to be built to the memory of the first thief and the first prostitute.'

"To equate them to the Unknown Soldier?"

"Yes, and I assure you it would be an act of great courage. Maybe it would give everyone food for thought."

The Keeper smiled. I didn't know if he agreed with me or not. He said he was glad that I had graced his lunch with him. I replied that he had fasted and I was sorry. The Keeper, as was his habit, rolled his eyes and spread his arms.

"Do you know what we used to call our dear brother from Bologna?"

"The one with the tortellini?"

"Yup. He had a name, so to speak, in code: Jesus. »

He looked at me to see how I reacted. I gave him no satisfaction. As if he had suddenly remembered some important news, he said to me: «By the way, your friend Giulia Lazzari is in Paris and she's fine. They tell me that she will have a boy.'

I didn't ask him how he knew, he wasn't going to tell me. I thought he was dismissing me, instead he looked at me with sympathy and observed that I had ability, intelligence, strength and could be useful to his project.

"What's your plan?"

«The result of the weapons is momentary, hatred instead exists. These words should be engraved on the door of every foreign ministry. The Cousins of the Wall want Jerusalem as the capital of the Jewish state, like today. Friends of the Rock want East Jerusalem as their capital. My project is to work to the hypothesis of Jerusalem Old city of peace, whose balance is guaranteed by the various religions.

"What does it actually mean, Reverend Father? That we, the Orthodox, the Jews, the Muslims would rule the Old City?"

The Keeper smiled fondly.

"I take it you've been on the topmost terrace of the

Tower of David."

"Yes, Reverend Father."

"And what did he think?"

«That the panorama is unique, because I can see Our Lord, Mohammed and the God of the Jews next to each other, and imagine that they are one God.»

«Father Matteo, you have stumbled over the truth. You don't act like most human beings who get up and go on their way."

I watched him in silence. I was beginning to understand.

"Jerusalem must be taken away from politics and arms and returned to God, right?"

"Yup."

"And do you agree with the leaders of the other churches?"

«We are working in this direction. But people like you are needed to keep watch."

I replied that I appreciated the esteem towards me but I had not even managed to save the life of that Melkite patriot. He made a face, perhaps of disapproval, and said: «He freed Giulia Lazzari, and it wasn't easy. I assure you that Saul Bialik had no desire to let you go. You have shown your wit and ability.'

From that moment on, I decided not to ask myself how the Keeper knew so many things.

«You have religious and humanitarian principles, you feel them and you carry them inside. The story of Mustafà and mother mouse proves it.

I thought it wasn't the Keeper's style to pay so many compliments. He continued: 'In 1808 Napoleon wanted to conclude a treaty with Russia to put Austria in trouble. He summoned Tsar Alexander I to Erfurt and for that delicate mission on which the fate of his politics depended he was accompanied by Talleyrand. In Erfurt secretly Talleyrand met Alexander and encouraged him to resist Napoleon's pressure. Talleyrand knew he was in grave danger, he could have appeared a champion of duplicity, but he was inspired by a very high political rigor together with an ethical value".

He looked at me for a long time. I didn't reply because I didn't know what to say. The Keeper raised his head upwards, stared at the ceiling: "There will be a Chapter shortly."

"It wasn't expected at this time."

The Keeper said dryly, "I predicted it."

He added, "There aren't many forests, many rivers, many lakes in this country. There is only one river, the Jordan, for both. And only one lake which we call the Sea of Galilee and the Israelis Kinneret. Jesus walked on the Sea of Galilee. And he slept in Peter's house, which is in the village of Capernaum, on the shore of that sea. Kinneret is the national water reservoir for Israelis. The rise and fall of its level are experienced by them with attention and sometimes with anguish, due to the danger of drought».

He took a long pause.

«You will have to carry out containment missions with the aim of working for Jerusalem City of Peace. You will be a kind of mediator between all parties involved, including us. »

I exclaimed that it seemed like too much work for one person. And I reminded him of Francis' journey who, upon arriving in the Holy Land, went to see the sultan Melek el Kamel. He asked that access to the Holy Places be left free, he anticipated the idea that it would be better to try to convert non-Christians rather than fight them, he proposed a simple evangelizing presence that seeks dialogue with the Palestinians starting from the values expressed in the Gospel. First of all, universal love, aimed at every man, of whatever religion he was. At the same time Francis, as a practical man that he was, organized the installation of his friars and the birth of the Custody of the Holy Land. I concluded that I didn't dare compare myself to him.

«Me neither» smiled the Keeper, «but I humbly want to develop your ideas. Old Jerusalem is to be governed jointly by Muslims, Jews and Christians. Over Old Jerusalem there must be only the sovereignty of God and not of men. We Christians, with the mullahs and rabbis, will represent God and bring about peace. You don't have to worry about your containment missions. You will have something in your hand that will allow you to keep watch."

"What, Reverend Father?"

"He'll know when the time is right." It was at that point that I asked him if he knew the difference between a great actor and a leading actor. The Keeper looked at me astonished and nodded.

«When the first actor enters the scene, he is respected by all. From the public and from fellow workers. The great actor is the scene, while he acts the scene is modeled on him. He bats his eyelashes and the audience cries or laughs. You respect the leading actor, you love the great actor unconditionally, you listen attentively to the leading actor, the great actor lets your imagination fly. Reverend Father, do I look like a leading actor or a great actor to you?»

The Guardian laughed heartily and did not answer me. He said, "It seems there is a somewhat imprudent brother at the Holy Sepulchre. So whisper the bad tongues. He would like to resurrect the Intifada. I remind you that only Jesus resurrected the dead and it also cost him a certain amount of effort. Father Matteo, I entrust myself to his common sense to contain and monitor certain imprudence ».

The interview was over. I got the feeling the Keeper wasn't feeling well, but maybe I was wrong.

CHAPTER THREE MUHAMMAD

At that time I was dealing with the organization of the archaeological-biblical park of Mount Nebo. At the foot of the mountain, on the Jordan River, was the site of Jesus' baptism, and I had restored the shrine that commemorated it.

The Jordanian Minister of Tourism, when the Pope came to visit Nebo, had proudly recalled that Jesus had been baptized in Jordan and not in Israel. And the Cousins of the Wall, who had also crucified him but who cared about certain territorial prerogatives, were offended. In reality, Jesus had received the sacrament in the Jordan and the river flowed through the Holy Land. Only this was true. The rest concerned the controversies and constant teasing that Cousins of the Wall and Friends of the Rock exchanged. I feared that the task entrusted to me by the Keeper would cause many problems because the contours of him were undefined. Furthermore, he would have distracted me from my studies and my research. In the company of these not very reassuring thoughts, I returned to the Flagellation.
It was Muhammad's voice that brought me back to reality.

He was sitting in front of the door, on a capital that sooner or later I would have restored. Muhammad, a tall, good-looking man, graying moustache, deep black eyes, uncut Jerusalem blue suit, white shirt, bright red tie, was an old friend and commanded the place police station of the Temple Mount.

The last time I visited him, I entered through the Bab as Silsileh Gate. The Israeli soldiers on guard greeted me, one of them spoke to me in Hebrew, I replied in English, he replied in Hebrew saying that he knew who I was and that I knew his language, I smiled at him, he shook his head and he repeated that I understood Hebrew because I answered him in English, perhaps to offend him?

I had shrugged and walked over to Muhammad's office, a small white house near the Dome of the Rock mosque, and once again admired its square construction, its white outer walls decorated below with two rows of arabesque tiles with a blue background. The office door was ajar, I had entered. The place was small, there was a desk, a chair, a wardrobe, a sofa with flowers, on the walls the photos with dedications of the Grand Mufti of Jerusalem and Arafat, and, almost to do no one wrong, of Nasser and Burghiba , of Sadat and Gaddafi, of Mubarak and Assad, of Hussein and Saddam. Then with amazement I saw a new portrait, that of Moshe Dayan. On a tag under the frame was written: "The only sabra who has respected the pacts."

Muhammad hugged me, his eyes watered.:

"Margot has left me, she's gone back to Paris."

A very pained expression did not appear on my face because I knew Margot well and she had not seemed like a good wife. I had never told Muhammad. Instead, I asked him if she was in a lot of pain. He replied that he was very ill for three reasons. The first because he loved Margot, the second because his father, mother, sisters and brothers had never accepted a Christian wife. And what had happened proved them right. The third concerned the children. He could not allow the two boys to study in Paris. They were to be educated in Jerusalem.

"A family" he concluded "must live together with its traditions, traditions are like the roots of a tree, if you cut them you condemn the tree to death, dry its leaves and the nests fall."

We entered the courtyard. He followed me to the Coin Studio. I offered him a coffee. She sipped it with pleasure. He said she preferred it to the Turkish one.

I asked him how I could help him. He replied that, if I had a conference scheduled in Paris in the near future, I should have spoken to Margot and invited her to reflect, even though he knew very well how difficult any reasoning with her was. I promised. She thanked me for being available. I said, "They tell me the Israelis are hunting."

He replied, "They always go hunting."

"But this time the hare belongs to my family."

He looked at me questioningly. I explained that it was a Franciscan. Muhammad shrugged, he knew nothing and if he knew nothing neither did the Israelis. I asked who his friends were, Hamas, Hezbollah, Jihad, whether he was related to Arafat's people or Abu Nidal or Abu Abbas. He didn't answer.

I tried to insist. He assured me that one day he would reveal it to me.

"Muhammad, we have been here since 1219 and for eight hundred years we have guarded the holy places. But guarding them meant first of all redeeming them from you. And once redeemed, defend them even at the cost of life. No less than four thousand brothers have offered it and their sacrifice makes our presence even more necessary, fatal, ineluctable. The only solution is to live peace together and collaborate with Israelis and Palestinians. You have to help me."

"I," he coughed softly, "have other problems, like I told you."

"We live among problems in Jerusalem, but we trust in providence."

"It's a word that doesn't belong to me."

"Looks like the brother's passing information."

"To who?"

"To you."

"What does information mean? You know well that we inform each other all day long. I, Sunni, inform the Orthodox who informs the Armenian, who informs the Jew, who informs the Shiite, who informs the Druze, who informs the Melkite, who informs the Abyssinian who informs the Catholic, who again informs me ."

I replied that it was also a way to feel alive. And I added: «Muhammad, Jerusalem means City of Peace. We inform ourselves about peace and for peace. Have you been away from the Holy Sepulcher for a long time?».

"Yup. It's not my business, as you know."

"Please, when you can, go to the Holy Sepulcher to see how the faith of our people is expressed."

I remembered what the Keeper had told me before saying goodbye.

«The emotion is renewed in my heart every day, when in the evening I spend a few moments of my day following the procession of our friars in the Holy Sepulchre. And more and more I am convinced of the inescapable right of our people to venerate the relics of Our Lord. It is a happiness that no one should take away from us. That's why we're here and we always will be."

I smiled with an expression that amazed Muhammad.

"What are you thinking about?"

It was I who didn't answer him, then I asked him: "Are you coming to lunch in the refectory?"

"Do you accept an infidel?"

"But you're almost a convert."

"Look, we've been guarding the Door of the Holy Sepulcher since 1246."

«If we really want to respect the truth, you have the keys to the Door, we will guard the Holy Sepulchre.»

The refectory hall was full. We found seats on a bench in the center of the long table. The table was U-shaped and could accommodate a maximum of thirty brothers. I was greeted with great greetings by Father Luca, who had just arrived from Capernaum. Muhammad was comfortable with him and smiled at Luca, who was tall, strong and had a reputation for being a big eater. He shouted to Muhammad, "Infidel, do you like short pasta with potatoes?"
"I've never eaten it."

"After the first course," shouted Luca, who was deaf in one ear, but whom no one dared ask to lower his voice, "you will ask to become a Christian."

Muhammad's plate was filled twice and Luca also made him drink wine, shouting at him: "Infidel, by drinking wine you sin and you can't even confess."

Muhammad laughed happily. Luca took a breath, stared at him and said: «Now I'll tell you a good story. That of one of our brothers. His name was Girolamo Mihaic and he was the one who bought Mount Nebo where my pupil Matteo works. Jerome had become friends with the king of Jordan. And do you know how? He had known that the king liked fruit and so he began sending him baskets of bananas, peaches, apples, plums grown at our mission in Jericho. The fruit made a great impression on the king, it was a sign of homage but it was also sweet, juicy, very good. Jerome did not know which of the two peaks of Nebo, El-Mukhayyat and Siyagha, was that of Moses. And so in 1932 he bought them both. In those days it was impossible for a foreigner to buy lands in Jordan directly and Jerome used, I guess with the king's tacit consent, a figurehead, a Cyrenean from Madaba, Salameh Swakaath. It was always that fruit, of which the king had become very greedy, that allowed Jerome to overcome any bureaucratic difficulty by obtaining permission for the excavations, which were entrusted to the Studium Biblicum. There were three major campaigns in 1933, 1935 and 1937, directed by Silvestro Saller. It was Girolamo who took care of the expenses, except those for the excavations, which were Silvestro's responsibility.

One day, four policemen arrive in Siyagha. They come to see the place where Moses is buried. After a while, they organize a shooting contest. It's about hitting a dinar flying through the air. It is Jerome who throws it. None of the policemen holes the coin. Girolamo asks if he can try. The cops make fun of him. They've never seen a friar who shoots. Girolamo borrows a rifle from one of them, takes it up and without even taking aim, hits the dinar forcefully pulled by a policeman. They comment that it was just a fluke. Jerome hits all the coins one after the other which they, in turn, throw higher and higher. From that moment Girolamo was considered one of them, indeed, the best among them, and this made relations with the authorities easier.

Luca paused, chewed slowly on a piece of bread and then, with the tone of one who had a secret, said in a low voice to Muhammad: «Girolamo, as a young man, had led the life of a gaucho in the Argentine Pampas and there he had learned to shoot and ride a horse. At Nebo he thought of everything. At lunch there was always spaghetti arriving from Italy and fruit from Jericho. The bread was baked in Jerusalem and, when it ran out, guests and residents ate that of Madaba which was more elastic and with a few stones inside, because the wheat in those parts was ground in a primitive way".

Luca brought his face closer to Muhammad's: "Do

you understand, infidel, what race we Franciscans are made of?"

Muhammad replied that he had always admired the Franciscans and it was no coincidence that he considered me one of his best friends. A brother asked Luca:

«How is Carlino?».

Muhammad, trying to joke, said it was quite a ridiculous name for a friar. Luca yelled: «Carlino is my dog, infidel! A poor bastard, snatched a couple of years ago from a gang of boys of your religion who were playing ball with him.'

"In Capernaum?" Muhammad asked.

"Of course."

"Were they Jewish?"

"No, no, they were yours!" Luke exclaimed. "Poor Carlin. I took good care of him, he had many broken bones, his mouth was all bad, but he didn't complain. »

I intervened: «I've read a book that I recommend to you, Luca. The title is very serious: Centuries of darkness. A challenge to the traditional chronology of the old world».

Luca fell into my provocation by asking me what those shocking news were.

"Historians, according to the author, have calculated two hundred and fifty years that never existed and they blow all the accounts."

"Now I surprise you," said Luca. He looked at his watch.

"My accounts tell me it's getting late. I have to go back to Capernaum. That's the shocking news." She caressed the watch. «He never misses the century. When are you coming to see me, Matteo?»

"Soon," I replied.

«You too, infidel, if you want to see the stones on which Our Lord rested, are welcome.»

"Thank you," Muhammad replied without much enthusiasm.

Luca greeted us and got up from the table. We realized that we were alone in the refectory. Muhammad, as I accompanied him to the door, said to me: "As regards the information you asked me, yes, it is true, there is a friar of yours who is getting a bit too excited. The Israelis know this and the Palestinians too. It seems to me that he is at the Holy Sepulchre.'
"Do you think so or is it so?"

"You know that relations in Jerusalem are complex. I trust your common sense."
Then as he shook my hand he looked up at the sky.

"I feel there will be a lot of snow this winter. And the years with the most snow are also the years with the most olives."

He embraced me, I saw him walking away along the Via Dolorosa. He walked stooped and sad. Luca with his somewhat heavy humor would have said to him: «You see, infidel, the way is painful for you too».

CHAPTER FOUR SYLVESTER

From an architectural point of view, the Holy Sepulcher is the least fascinating place in Jerusalem. I have declared it in many conferences and once the Custos also addressed me an unofficial reminder, let's call it that.

The pope was about to arrive and I was interviewed by an Italian television correspondent in my capacity as a Franciscan archaeologist. When there was the question about the restructuring of the dome of the Holy Sepulcher I indulged in a series of considerations regarding the Orthodox brothers which certainly did not please some in Rome. The conclusion of my reasoning was that the Orthodox patriarch and his small court of incompetents were primarily responsible for that disaster. The Custos summoned me and in the presence of the Latin patriarch's secretary he said to me: «There is a rumor going around about a secret clause of the Islamic Conference which would commit Muslim countries to expel all Christians from the Middle East. Western experts consider this rumor to be nonsense.

The Latin patriarch's secretary, a grayish-skinned Dominican with watery eyes, nodded seriously.

"It's a difficult skein even for the pope," continued the Guardian, "don't set yourself up as a sapper. Leave the Orthodox alone, they're so touchy.'

Despite the rebuke, my impression was that the Custos agreed with me and had recited in front of the patriarch's secretary. As far as Rome was concerned, she was a long way away and the pope had other concerns.

I entered the paved courtyard in front of the basilica and a bearded brother more or less my age came towards me, smiling. His name was Silvestro and he had taken me for a tourist. No one usually noticed that I was a friar. The only one who had been an exception was Giulia Lazzari.

He explained to me how the iron grille that I saw in front of me protected the epitaph of Philip d'Aubigny and, of the two twin doors, the one on the right had been walled up since the time of Saladin and the custody of the other belonged by ancient privilege to two Muslim families. One kept the keys, the other the right to open.

"Thus," he concluded, "the Friends of the Rock have controlled the tomb of Our Lord since 1246."

Silvestro had spoken quickly and with a strong Sicilian accent. I thanked him for his attention and did not tell him that I taught the story he had told me at the university in a more complex and in-depth way, and I often spent pleasant evenings in the Muslim quarter as guests of the family that kept those keys. Silvestro said: "You don't look like a pilgrim to me."
"Indeed."
"Do you live around here?"
"A few months out of the year."
«I have never seen her at the Holy Sepulchre. Atheist?"
"No, Catholic."

Silvestro was in charge of the officiation of the basilica and gave assistance to the pilgrims, accompanied them to visit the Calvary, the Sepulcher and the other Sacred Places.

«Come with me, I'll show you our convent, even if in reality it isn't possible, it's an exception to the rule, but you inspire me trust and sympathy.»
We entered the Franciscan chapel.

"It is consecrated to the Apparition of Our Lord to Mary" said Silvestro, "the Gospel does not speak of it but

tradition has transmitted its memory."
Behind the chapel was the little convent which of course
I knew well.
"They are very old walls," he explained to me, "they
breathe the memory of the Crusaders."

His cell was spacious. She told me she lived in
happiness and showed me a photo album. The subject, a
flamenco dancer. He asked me who I thought that
dancer was. It was clear that it was him, but I shrugged
and shook my head. Silvestro told me about a vacation
he had many years earlier in Seville. He had become
friends with a boy who had introduced him to his
family. He had little money and so he had gladly
accepted the invitation to live in that house. He was in
the gypsy quarter which came to life extraordinarily at
night. They sang, they danced. The friend had a sister.
She taught him to dance and that's how he became a
flamenco dancer. They formed a couple. They were
quite successful and loved each other very much. Then
there was the accident. After a show in Pamplona. He
was driving, she died: instantly. He remained between
life and death for several days. He made a vow: if he
survived he would become a friar. Silvestro sighed for a
long time and then gravely affirmed: «What is folded
becomes whole. What is crooked becomes straight.
What is worn out becomes new."
"Lao Tzu."
He looked at me astonished: «Have you read it?».
"Yup."
"Then you will understand the continuation of my
story."

She entered the convent in Assisi. But after a while
the desire to spend what remained of his earthly
existence at the Holy Sepulcher invaded him. Our Lord

granted him. He was transferred from Assisi to Jerusalem. He, the humblest and most impure of all the Franciscans, with a belated and sudden vocation, would have lived every day and every night in the Holy City, the place of martyrdom and resurrection. If happiness existed, he considered himself truly happy. Sylvester's eyes shone. He spoke to me of the power of the Gospel, of its flavor of salvation for man who still today can and must identify himself with the healed paralytic, the repentant Magdalene, Peter's forgiveness.

«Within man stirs the same renewal, the same rebirth, the same hope of the days of Our Lord's earthly preaching. The Lord knows the heart of man. He knows how to move and take it, he can give it the strength and feeling of original innocence. »

That evening we went to a small Greek restaurant in the Christian Quarter for dinner. I don't like Greek cuisine, it smells too much of yoghurt and feta cheese. I ordered a salad with tomatoes, Silvestro swallowed two portions of fat and heavy moussaka with joyous voracity.

He also drank Cyprus wine, maybe too much, his eyes became watery. She heaved a long sigh. And he said he could talk to me well.

Friendships are sometimes born in a burning way and run with love. Silvestro was strong-willed, authentic in feelings and had his own personal relationship with religion. Perhaps questionable, but sincere. It was I who hadn't been honest with him. In his mind, Taoism and Catholicism seemed bizarrely united, but I understood the thread. His was an absolute faith in a justice that should privilege and save the most defenseless, children, the poor, the old. And in Jerusalem, Palestinian children were also poor.

I liked Silvestro, I admired his patience, his joy in

explaining every corner of the basilica to pilgrims. He told me that I had to consider him a brother who loved his brothers and did not want to suffer the faith as if it were a bureaucracy.

He invited me to his mass. He celebrated in the chapel of the Apparition. I saw many boys and at the end of the ritual Silvestro spoke in a low voice to them, he seemed to give orders like a coach to his team. He noticed my questioning look, he took my arm, he would explain to me.

I accompanied him to a somewhat dirty and dark café on the Via Dolorosa. We sat down at a table where one person was waiting for us. Silvestro managed to amaze me again. He was a young Israeli soldier. They had met at the Holy Sepulchre. The soldier had sprained his ankle, a trivial accident. Silvestro had helped him, treated him, a kind of friendship was born. Every now and then the soldier went to see him and they drank coffee together.

Silvestro introduced me as a friend who lived in Jerusalem, then he stopped and maybe, realizing that he knew nothing else about me, he gave me a questioning look, but he decided it wasn't the time for explanations. The soldier started talking about the girlfriend who had left him for someone else, a Sabra from Haifa, he was a Sephardic from Tel Aviv. Silvestro listened to her pains and pitied him. And then, having finished with the speech of heartbreaks, he wanted to know if he was always a sniper. That he said yes, and that the orders to open fire changed often and even several times in the course of a day. He was happy when orders were moderate.

"What does moderate mean?" asked Sylvester.

«An individual who throws a Molotov cocktail must be wounded in the legs, but if he is also armed he can be shot in the upper parts of the body. Every dead person is photographed. So we can prove that it's not a child and that he had a weapon."

"Palestinians say you kill a lot of children."

It was I who was speaking now, the soldier either didn't notice or considered it a negligible fact. He replied: «It is difficult to say, there can be mistakes, a child can be killed by mistake. Yes, it can happen."

"What is a mistake? The rifle that fires itself?" I pressed.

He didn't take the provocation and replied calmly: «I see a boy who is moving in a strange way, perhaps he wants to pick up a stone or something similar. I ask my commander to shoot. The commander tells me, if you think he's suspicious, he shoots to scare him.'

"Then?"

"It's windy, the rifle moves a few millimeters, I'm going through his head."

"For error."

"Of course it was a mistake," the soldier replied nervously.

"But why kill, not just hurt?" Silvestro asked and the soldier replied in a slightly bored tone, as if it were a topic already addressed in other meetings.

«I already explained it to you once, Silvestro. If you hurt an individual, he will scream and shout that you have hurt him. I have a settler friend and he says that every time they shoot, we have to kill them. If you were talking to him, the conversation would be completely different. But you're talking to me and my conscience suggests moderation."

"Did your conscience allow you to shoot children?" I asked.

"I've never shot children."

Sylvester wanted to know why he was so sure.

"Because from the age of twelve on, an individual is no longer a child."

"Who set it up?" asked Sylvester.

"My bosses. They say that after the age of twelve one is no longer a child."

"Does that seem logical to you?"

Perhaps my tone was aggressive because Jonas – that was his name – turned to me with irritation: «But who are you? And why are you asking me all these questions?"

Silvestro replied that I wanted to know his soul better. Jonas replied:

"My rabbi takes care of my soul. You took care of my ankle and I'm grateful, but I don't feel like talking about my work with a stranger.'

Silvestro told him he was right and apologized. I was a friend anyway. The soldier seemed to calm down. He said he had to go and they would see each other the following week. Leaving the café, he muttered to Silvestro, pointing at me: "I still haven't figured out who that guy is."

Silvestro smiled at me and then said: «I wanted you to listen. Now I can answer your question."

"I didn't speak."

"But your eyes do."

He took my arm, we walked along the Via Dolorosa. She told me he knew he could trust me. She took a breath. When there was a demonstration by the Friends of the Rock against the Cousins of the Wall, the Israeli policemen used to hit the heads of the Palestinian boys with their batons to make them stupid, and their arms and legs to cripple them. And since his catechism students wanted to participate actively in that painful and endless urban struggle against settlers and fundamentalists, he had trained them to puncture tyres, to put water in petrol, to ruin enemy cars in every way. The boys moved at night in groups of three, and the Israelis had never managed to capture one. Silvestro concluded satisfied, as if it were a bulletin of war, that his people had already damaged ten cars and eight motorcycles and were now planning a full-scale action using the full squad. The results, he proudly explained to me, he found entirely positive. His "boys from via Paal" were happy because they actively participated in the struggle and studied catechism like good Christians. Then he added, "You saw the torment of that soldier."

"It seemed to me that he agonized more for his fiancée than for the bullets."

Sylvester did not reply and concluded: «The desert will have to become a garden and in the garden law and justice will reign».

That evening I had dinner with some American archaeologists, but I was distracted. What was I going to tell the Keeper? That one of his friars was pursuing justice and law, organizing a very personal guerrilla war?

I believed in every peace proposal, in every negotiation. And when politics and interests are at stake, a favorable outcome is possible. But it takes faith and generosity. If religion is the protagonist, generosity is killed by faith because one fights for a rock where a religion claims that Mohammed stopped to pray. On that rock Abraham almost killed Isaac, and Hiram of Tire built the Temple for Solomon in the likeness of the House of God. On that rock, a thousand years later, nine Templars lived to discover the secrets of that perfect building whose origins lay in the heavenly conversation of God with Moses. And today the Jews wept over the only remaining wall of their Temple and the Muslims venerated that rock on which the wall rested.

In those few meters the destinies of two great religions were consummated, and those few meters were worth more than a thousand oil wells. Religions bring discord, I thought. Religions were born not to coexist, otherwise everyone would pray to the same God. A believer kills another believer to honor the same God, but that sacred name is pronounced differently. The wars of religion, concluded, arise from a question of language. And Silvestro, with all his intelligence and goodness, moved like a blind man.

I went to see the Keeper. He was pleased that I had accepted his invitation to visit the Sepulcher with such enthusiasm.

«Unfortunately» he sighed sadly, «inside the basilica there are at least five Christian denominations that exercise divine office there, it is an example of the division that exists between us. Yet Our Lord had said: "Love one another as I have loved you". Today's situation makes mutual charity very difficult. Charity must be able to overcome every barrier. It takes patience, one must not disturb the order. It is a precarious, uncertain order, but uncertainty too has its rules. You agree, don't you?"

I told him yes.

"I know you met some of our brothers."

I replied that I had met Silvestro and told him the whole story of his conversion and how for him the greatest joy, the sublime experience of faith was to live in the Holy Sepulchre.

«I was unaware of this aspect of Father Silvestro's life. Faith is truly something mysterious. But obedience is not mysterious."

I wondered, without giving me a convincing answer, if I had been right in not revealing the whole interview to him. The Keeper ran his hands through his hair, grimaced in pain. I was uncertain whether to say something to him or ignore his gesture. I decided to participate in the intimacy of him.

"Are you not feeling well, Reverend Father?"

"Dogs that bark, that's the problem," he replied.

I was dumbfounded. He continued: «This is how Pius IX defined the Jews and they remember it. If instead of that phrase, if instead of barking dogs we could say other words, maybe..."

«After so many years, are we reinterpreting Pius IX?»

"Faith and patience know no bounds."

"Shall we change history, Reverend Father?"

«If we tried to explain that the dogs that bark are not only Jews but all those who have no faith, we could also include a few Christians, Muslims, Buddhists. All those who apparently profess a religion and do so without committing themselves. We could say that this was Pius IX's thought.»

"Perhaps we could work on this idea."

"There are already people working there," the Keeper finished dryly. After a long pause he added, 'I'm not very well, I guess you've noticed. Father Matteo, in the next chapter you will be appointed Discreet and will take care of cultural affairs.'

In our environment the Discretum is part of the Discretorium, a sort of council of ministers. There are six Discretes. Each one represents a linguistic community: Italian, English, French, German, Spanish, Arabic. I would have become the Discreet of the Italian community, the most numerous. As far as work assignments are concerned, each of the elected members makes their experience available and then decides by mutual agreement. This time it was the Keeper who had decided, I guess without consulting anyone, that I would take care of cultural affairs. But who could question the legitimacy of that choice?

"I hope you enjoy the assignment," the Keeper observed with mild irony.

"Sure," I exclaimed as enthusiastically as possible.

I was about to get up. The Keeper looked at me as if the interview wasn't over yet.

"Does Raed remember that?"

"Yup."

"They shot him."

"Is dead?"

"Already."

CHAPTER FIVE MERCY AND PROVIDENCE

I walked back to the Flagellation as usual. It was late, the shops closed, the shutters down, nobody was there. I carried with me a feeling of sadness and abandonment also due to the attitude of the Guardian. He hadn't told me everything that was on his mind. And the next assignment filled me with perplexity. I should have been happy to go Discreet but instead I thought it would mean more politics and less mosaics. And this could not happen. Through archeology I was getting closer to God. The Keeper knew it. That's why I was more amazed than flattered by his decision.

Once, at the end of a conference, someone stood up and asked me if I had become a priest to become an archaeologist. I replied that the two vocations were born together. Now, thinking back on those words of mine, I realized that I wasn't so sure after all. And I couldn't answer myself, as I had always done, that by digging and restoring I was praying, and my work in search of Christian origins made me feel good. It was not like this. Not that I had any faith issues, in fact, I found 'my relationship with religion rich in innocence. But sometimes things happened that disturbed me. Like Raed's.

Years ago I was walking back to the Flagellation from the Jaffa Gate. There were the usual tourists, the usual pilgrims, the usual hate in the air.

I was at the Tower of David when from the road that bordered the Armenian quarter I saw a child running towards me. I don't know if he was smiling or sulking, maybe he had mistaken me for someone else, but I felt it as an act of trust in me. In those few moments I felt affection and tenderness for him. He was about a meter away from me when I heard a sharp thud, then sudden silence. The child's run ended up in my arms which had opened automatically. His blood flowed slowly and softly from a tiny hole in his shirt, at the height of his right shoulder. I immediately accompanied him to the hospital. The wound wasn't serious, and Raed, that was his name, recovered. We could not figure out who shot him. I left for Paris and when I returned Raed had been discharged from the hospital and was a guest of the Custody. The family lived in Jericho, were very poor, and Raed was in a sense adopted by the Keeper at the time. The current one was then elected and Raed continued to live in San Salvatore and regularly attend school. One day he disappeared. And no one heard from him again.

Some time passed. I forgot about him. I was driving to Jericho one afternoon in a freezing, heavy rain when a rock struck the windshield of my car on the outskirts of the city. The car skidded on the slippery road, finally stopping inches from a cedar. I had risked my life. I touched my face, my neck, my chest. I wasn't hurt. It was then that I saw Raed. He had a stone in his hand, she was with other guys. He recognized me and as his friends fled he shouted at me:
"Get out".

I was standing in the rain, my hair wet, water running down my face. I tried to talk to him.

"I'm too busy right now," he shouted at me, checking the license plates of the cars that kept passing on that street. He had to figure out if they were blue, meaning Palestinian, or yellow, meaning Israeli. At the appearance of a Fiat with yellow number plates he threw the stone at him. The throw was too short and the stone rolled on the asphalt without causing any damage.

"It hasn't been a good afternoon," she sighed. "I didn't damage any cars."

I replied that he had ruined mine. She said she was sorry because I was a friend. The siren of a police vehicle made his prospects for the day even worse. She fled into the dirt lanes where they certainly wouldn't have chased her, I continued on foot along the main road. I went into a fruit and vegetable shop. I bought an apple and a banana. I was hungry. I ate them right away. When I came out, Raed was across the street, in front of an abandoned building, waving for me to follow. Tripping over the rubbish and debris of ruined houses, after a few hundred yards we came to a metal door. Raed knocked softly, the door opened, two female hands pulled him inside, and in an instant they tore off his wet jacket, changing it for a dry one of a different color,

"This is my mother Rahme," he said, pointing to the smaller of the two women. "And this is my other mother, Fatin. She's not exactly my mother, but she married my father after my mother."

At fifteen, Raed was the oldest of eight brothers and sisters. They all lived in that miserable house. The cold infiltrated the rough gray walls, the rain dripped from the holed roof. Raed's brothers had coughs and fevers. In the midst of that chaos, the women tried to be hospitable. As Rahme served me a frugal plate of rice-stuffed vine leaves, Raed related what he had never told me or the Keeper: "My grandmother once owned flocks of sheep and olive groves, and our family lived well."

He told me of the neat rows of fruit trees that glittered on the hillsides, of the lambs that grazed in the well-watered fields in spring, of the overflowing platters of freshly butchered meat at lunch and dinner. She had never seen the farm of which she had such a vivid image. His father had described it to him. During the Israeli War of Independence in 1948, his grandmother's family fled the place, and by Raed's birth it was a settlement of Jewish settlers.

Then he had been wounded in Jaffa, I had saved him, he had lived with us for a while and studied, and later returned to his own people. But he had been in prison before. For this he had disappeared from the Custody. They had arrested him for no apparent reason.

"The Israelis," he concluded, "have not been kind to me. First they shoot me and I don't know why, then they arrest me and I don't know why. Doesn't it seem logical to you, Father Matteo, that I throw stones at them?»

Raed walked me to the car. She walked fast, with long, nervous steps, the rain had stopped, the arid earth had absorbed her as if she had never fallen, the stones cleaned of the dust had turned white again. Somehow I managed to get the car going again. And I drove with a cracked windshield.

I didn't see him again for another year. One evening he showed up at the Flagellation. He was cheerful. He announced to me that he had found a job. The next day, in Jericho, he would begin a trial period as a croupier at the Casino. He told me that his friends in Hamas had denounced the "devil's casino," that's what they called it, but if he got the job, the salary would be four times what he could earn elsewhere.

"I know it's immoral," he said softly. "But do you think a dead man worries about being killed?" He wanted me to teach him poker and blackjack. I asked him how it came to his mind that a friar was an expert in cards. And he candidly replied that I knew how to do everything for him. We worked most of the night. Raed didn't even know the names of the suits and the courts.
"This is the ace of hearts," I explained.

"Is that shape called a heart?" he asked surprised. And then he concluded, "It looks like a slice of meat to me."

It was the last time I saw him.

"Ayden melton!"

The firm, almost hostile tone roused me from my thoughts. I realized that I had crossed the Old City without realizing it and was on the Via Dolorosa, a few dozen meters before the Flagellation. Someone came at me and tried to hit me and instinctively I defended myself. We rolled to the ground. It was only a moment, because immediately afterwards Silvestro embraced me crying and asked forgiveness for the attack. I hugged him too and when he had calmed down I told him that maybe it would be better to go for a walk and talk. He exclaimed excitedly: «They are kicking me out. I abandon my boys and Our Lord. I have become a dead man who was denied even Purgatory».

I breathe. He was calmer now.

"It's your fault, Father Matteo, that you didn't tell me you were one of ours." As I answered him, I understood that these were not the words he expected from me.

"Don't be surprised. In Jerusalem, relations are complex. I relied on common sense."

"Do you think you are a good priest?"

"I try hard to be."

"You tricked me." I searched for an explanation. I had none. He was right.

"You are one of ours," he insisted, "you made me speak and then you went to the Keeper, you told him everything and now the Keeper sends me into exile."

I couldn't tell him the truth. I asked him when he had met the Keeper. He replied that it was not important, I told him that I had to know.

"In the afternoon," and added, "He wants me to leave tomorrow. He said to me: "Go and spread your wings in Cyprus". »

I did something that seemed absurd but it wasn't. I accompanied him to visit my museum, I showed him the most beautiful pieces, the models of the excavations, the bas-reliefs, the mosaics. So, while I was showing him the collection of funerary busts from Palmyra, the pieces of a marble frieze that decorated the Edicule of the Holy Sepulchre, and I was explaining to him the origin of the various finds, his anger subsided, he asked me questions, I gave answers. He was moved in front of the colored fragments of the plaster of Peter's house in Capernaum, where Jesus had slept, and he asked me if he could touch them. I told him yes. Tears filled his eyes. He thanked me, now he had the strength to leave. I replied that it was a terrible test of faith. He wanted to pray in front of the sacred plaster.

We went up to the Study of Coins. I showed him my books and the photographs of the last mosaics I had excavated at Umm-er-Rasas, I told him about Mount Nebo and its sunsets and about the Promised Land that Moses saw from there and which has remained a promise to this day. And finally I asked him: "Have you ever visited Ginostra?"
"No."

"I was born there. It is the wildest part of Stromboli. Its few houses are attached to the cone of the volcano, there is a small church with a terrace in front of it and the sea overhanging below. Opposite are the other islands, Panarea, Vulcano, Lipari, Salina, Alicudi, Filicudi, and you can see them all. The port of Ginostra is called Pertuso, it is the smallest in the world, in addition to the Rollo, a maximum of three boats can enter. The ship from Naples stops a few hundred meters from the Pertuso. The Rollo, whose crew is made up of three people, the helmsman and two sailors, arrives under the ship and loads goods and passengers. When the sea is rough the Rollo does not leave the Pertuso. It happens often and I believe that this fact has had a great influence on the spirit and mood of us from Ginestre. We know the taste of isolation.

My father was the helmsman of the Rollo. Our house was halfway up the hill. There was a large vegetable garden, an olive grove, a chicken coop, an orchard, a considerable quantity of prickly pears.

The volcano offered constant energy. His warm and continuous muttering was a faithful companion at various times of the day.

A small colony of foreigners had settled in Ginostra who had bought the houses of the emigrants. For those who loved total isolation and considered Ginostra too inhabited, there was Lazzaro. Lazzaro was reached by following a path that passed under our house, dug between the prickly pear plants and the rock.

The Solomons lived in Lazarus. Husband and wife from Palermo, childless, spent half the year on the island. She was a retired teacher, he had a business that allowed him long vacations. On Sunday evening the Salomones, the doctor, the owner of the only shop in Ginostra where you could find almost everything, from pasta to vegetables and fruit, but not meat, and the two sailors who worked with my father, Carmelo and Santo , they came to our house for dinner. Santo was small in stature, thin, agile, with red hair. Carmelo was tall and robust. Santo was not married, Carmelo had a wife and children in Lipari and suffered from being away.

Mrs. Solomon was in her fifties, her hair was white and messy. She often made an impatient gesture with her hand to brush back a long strand that fell on her forehead. I had asked her, somewhat flippantly, why she didn't avoid that annoyance with the help of a pair of bobby pins. But she didn't answer me. Her blue eyes were large and dull and a little tired, her face wrinkled and sallow.

Signora Salomone was sarcastic and witty and only a fool could have been offended also because she was always willing to accept a joke of equal weight from her interlocutor. My mother was a specialist in this game and when she answered her Mrs Solomon's lips curled in a wide smile and her eyes watered. She was very nice to me. She amused me at her goofy face and the fact that she cared so little about her looks.

Her hair wasn't the only messy thing about her looks. Mrs Solomon was messy from head to toe. She usually alternated between a green blouse and a red one. Her top two unbuttoned buttons showed a wrinkled neck. Her blouse always had ash stains because Signora Salomone smoked a lot. The hems of her skirts were frayed and her shoes were brown even though she was wearing a black skirt. Yet to my eyes, and not only mine, she seemed full of charm and even elegant.

Playing scientific scopone with Mrs. Solomon was fun and instructive. He was fast, he combined flair with experience. The teamwork with her husband was admirable. Mr Solomon was solid and cautious and so his wife could allow herself to be bold and brilliant with a certain margin of safety. My father and Santo lost every Sunday and my father said every time: "I really don't know what's wrong with these cards. We manage to lose even when they are all good".

"I don't think it's his fault," Mrs. Solomon replied, looking him straight in the face with those pale blue eyes of hers. "It must be pure and simple bad luck. Of course, if he hadn't confused the queen of clubs with the queen of diamonds in the last hand, he would have saved the game."

Mr. Solomon was a man of medium height, with a shiny bald head, wiry gray mustache and gold-rimmed glasses. He almost always wore white canvas slacks and a blue T-shirt. Unlike Mrs Solomon he was very neat. He spoke little, and it was clear that he appreciated his wife's caustic wit.

One Sunday evening, when the Solomons after winning as usual took the path to Lazarus, my father, who didn't want to sleep, told me this story.

"You must know that I met Signora Salomone more than twenty years ago. She was always messy and sloppy, but when she was young her sloppiness didn't bother her, on the contrary she was even fascinating. She was married to a certain engineer Mancuso who managed a property near Castel di Tusa. At that time I was living in Lipari. I remember like it was yesterday the first time I saw her. There were still no cars on Lipari and Mr and Mrs Mancuso got off the ship by bicycle. Mrs. Mancuso was thinner than today, she had a beautiful complexion and a lot of dark hair. »

"I didn't see her again for almost twenty years" continued my father "and I was surprised when, having moved from Lipari to Ginostra, I met her in our church. She had changed a lot. He asked me: 'How are you? Do you remember me?'
'Of course' I replied.

'It's been a while since we last saw each other. We are no longer kids. Have you already met Signor Salomone?'

For a moment I didn't know who he was talking about. I had to make a very silly face, because he let out a smirk that I knew very well and explained to me: 'I married Mr Solomon. It was the best solution. I was a

widow and he insisted.'
'And Mr. Mancuso?'
'Died in an accident,' he replied dryly. 'I'm sorry, I hope you are happy today.' 'Delighted, he is a treasure'."

My father's story left me with a lot of curiosity. I would have liked to ask Signora Salomone why she spent so much time in Ginostra. But I never had the courage.

The life of all of us went on in a simple way, punctuated by the sun, the dark and the Sunday scientific scopone until the night that Salvo disappeared. They searched everywhere for him, until his body was found on the rocks halfway between Lazarus and Ginostra.

I was very affected by that incident. I didn't understand how Salvo, who was very agile, had slipped. It wasn't a particularly dangerous spot. One night I hid near the Solomons' house. An intuition, let's call it that. The Solomons were on their terrace facing the sea. They talked, she told him it had been an accident, he cried and replied that her jealousy had forced him to push Salvo onto the rocks. She caressed him and they cried together and then she told him a sentence that has remained imprinted in my memory: "You followed the feeling of love. And sometimes it kills."

I walked away very upset. That desperate couple had Moved me and I never revealed to anyone that they were murderers. I became, with my silence, their accomplice.

It was to atone for my guilt that I chose to dedicate myself to the Lord. Later, meeting Father Luca brought me happiness. But I want to tell you something important, Silvestro. With the priesthood and with archeology for me what is folded becomes whole and what is consumed becomes new.»

Silvestro hugged me for a long time with tears in his eyes. I really was his brother now. He slept in the Coin Study. Early the next day, I accompanied him to the airport. We embraced very tenderly and it was he who said to me:

"The Lord keep you."

As he left, I thought of a sentence I had read somewhere: "God is the place of the world, but very often the world is not His place."

CHAPTER SIX THE SHEIK

I returned from the airport to Jerusalem in the car of an old Jewish friend, Manfred Gerstenfeldt. He came from Rome. He often went to Italy as a consultant for the State Railways. He was an expert in rail transport and, in addition to Italy, had a contract with the Japanese and Australian railways. We rarely met, but we shared mutual sympathy and esteem. He told me that Israel was changing. There was no longer the passion of the past, the Founding Fathers had died with their ideals and their dreams. I replied that there was a lack of goodwill in the Israelis and the Palestinians. Manfred was annoyed and told me that good will had nothing to do with law. He exclaimed that he had the right to go and visit the grave of his father who survived in Dachau, which was located in the Jewish cemetery on the Mount of Olives. But there was a Palestinian village up there and the village boys' greatest amusement was throwing stones at those who knelt in front of their loved ones. Where was the goodwill? I wonder. So he and his son went to the Mount of Olives armed to defend their right. They pulled out their guns. They were shooting in the air. The Palestinian boys got scared and let them pray in peace. Conclusion: fear kept law alive.

Now he had a problem: he had to move his mother Jeannie's body to Jerusalem and place it next to his father's. But just the idea of being stone-thrown offended him. And he insulted the memory of a heroine. I asked him why his mother hadn't lived in Jerusalem. She replied that after her father's death she had returned to Paris because she was French, while her father was Dutch. She was a curious woman Jeannie, she had fought for Israel but she said she could not live there. And he, when he went to Rome for work, always found a way to rush to Paris to spend a few hours with her.

"She was extraordinary!" Manfred had tears in his eyes. «Matteo, I have to bury her next to him. He asked me before he died. Do you think I can tolerate that there is someone who dares to throw stones at my two heroes?»

I didn't know what to answer him. He left me at the Damascus Gate and pointing out to me the many Friends of the Rock who went out, entered, bought, talked, he said to me:
"Remember, whoever wins, however he won, feels no shame. And we are the winners."

I went back to the Flagellation thoughtfully. I realized that my life had been happy and lucky. Now she would have been less calm, but perhaps it was a test that the Lord was putting me through. Too much pain all at once, but if providence wanted it, at the end of the journey I would certainly have found myself better.

I was reminded of a Cousins of the Wall song I had recently heard whose lyrics went something like this: "When the rabbi sings, all the Hasidim sing. When the rabbi dances, all the Hasidim dance. When the rabbi drinks,all the Hasidim drink. When   to the Temple Mount to see Muhammad. He was in a good mood. He had talked to Margot and found a solution for her children. They would study in an Islamic school in Paris and spend their holidays with him. She congratulated me on my ability to solve Sylvester's case. The Guardian knew, the Israelis knew. But nobody wanted and could create a scandal.
"And you offered the solution by discovering that friar's secret."
"But I haven't told anyone about it."

"You went to see the Keeper."

"So?"

"He understood. And he convinced the Israelis that it was useless to arrest him. He would have punished him by taking him away from the Holy Sepulcher and from his boys. »

The Israelis, realizing once again how strange the religion of the Gentiles was, had accepted. The Custos, thanks to me, had saved Silvestro's life and the good name of the Custody. With the move to Cyprus he had offered his friar a lesson in discipline. Even the Palestinians had approved of this solution. Muhammad patted me affectionately on the shoulder: "You were good."

The next day I received an urgent message from Guillermo. The Keeper was waiting for me after dinner. I had been invited to the American Colony restaurant by two rather boring Italian embassy officials. Their only topic of conversation involved organizing a weekend in Damascus to buy carpets and rare antiques from an Iraqi opponent of Saddam who had taken refuge in the Syrian capital. They wanted advice from me. I was vague and generic. I walked along the walls of the Old City. There were the stars and a lot of calm and I thought once more that in Jerusalem with a little good will it would have been possible to live better than we do now. The air was fresh and pleasant, and I felt ready to face the Reverend Father.

Guillermo greeted me with a big smile and accompanied me to the Guardian's study. He was reading some mail. He didn't look up. He was abrupt.

"Is it late for you?"

"No," I replied.

"He's been doing well."

"And that satisfies you?"

"I would say yes. And now I am convinced that you are in a position to work even better."

He rolled his eyes, as was his habit. I was once so disrespectful.

"Don't tell me it was God's will."

"No, Jesus's."

"It's the same will."

"Indeed."

"I don't understand."

«Father Matteo, that Melkite wanted to die to save his child. And Jesus helped him. Father Sylvester made a mistake and Jesus had understanding for him."

I raised my voice and didn't call him Reverend Father.

"One is dead, the other is in exile. Is this called understanding?"

"And mercy too."

"What about Raed?"

"Despair."

I observed that it seemed to me a terrible lack of respect for God. He stared at me for a long time in silence. I didn't understand that look. The silence was lasting too long. It was I who spoke first. I was calmer.

«Reverend Father, I have never told you anything about Silvestro. How did you figure that out?"

«My friend, sometimes chance is identified with providence. His eyes were the case. »

"And providence?"

"Every word said about a material object is idle gossip."

"So?"

"Death hides in copious speeches."

"I don't understand."

"I never taught anything until I put it into practice." I didn't reply and he continued: «I hope I don't have to explain to you who Positheus of Gaza, Ephrem the Syrian, Barsanufio, Eugene are. They were all looking for the Holy Impassibility».

"I suppose the Reverend Father wants me to understand something."

And at this point I really admired him. He stood up and exclaimed: «Those sweet and frightening monks, those elusive and unclassifiable desert fathers, howled: the love of man takes us away from the love of God. They felt abandoned by God if they passed a few days without the torment of diseases. In one night some recited all one hundred and fifty Psalms with antiphons and hallelujah, still others stood with their hands raised from sunset to dawn. Others, praying and humbling themselves in every way, as well as driving out demons, wanted to obtain the remission of the sins of an entire generation, still others asked for the growth of wheat in every corner of the world". I asked him: «Reverend Father, there is a thought that runs inside me and concerns me

Saul Bialik. Was it he who told her about Silvestro?'

Smiling and dismissing me, he replied: «Go and re-read the lives of those fathers, I am convinced that you will feel more responsible and maybe they will even give you some miracle».

And yet my life was not entirely absorbed by the Keeper and the events that concerned him. The knowledge I had of Jerusalem and the Holy Land had allowed me to render some service to friends who asked for help, advice. But I tried to be thrifty with my availability, because first of all, in my heart and in my head, came excavations and prayer.I went to see, responding to his invitation, Monsignor Lahan, the Melkite bishop of Jerusalem. I maintained ancient relationships of custom and friendship with him. I walked through the little Melkite church, the walls darkened with age, the floors freshly mopped, and tenderly observed old men and women praying. Bishop Lahan offered me grapefruit juice, he was sitting at his desk, facing me. He rang the phone, picked up the receiver, listened in silence. Then he shook his head and said, "Rabbi Shach wants to revive the fight against non-religious Zionist and socialist movements. And so the hate continues. The plant of rights and the flower of justice will never grow in our garden. Many of my Melkites in '48 were forced to leave their villages and found themselves refugees in the fields of Lebanon. Others fled Jerusalem in 1967 and went to Jordan and Syria waiting to return to their homes. We live in a situation of political and social injustice, we have the problem of daily food, sometimes we use the strike, sometimes stones, sometimes newspapers. The cost of repression seems high only to us. According to the Israelis we should leave.'

"Where is it?"

"In the Dead Sea, perhaps. Forgive me for the outburst. I consider her a friend. You tried to help someone dear to me, Pascal Aretz."

"Did you also know Giulia Lazzari?"

"Yup."

"He's in Paris."

"I know, widowed and not quiet."

"Because?"

He ignored my question.

"You have to help me. They stole two precious antique candlesticks from our church."

"Who?"

«I don't know exactly, but a person they call the Sheikh is certain of the theft. He lives near the Nebo.

Near his house, I think. The candlesticks are not of great value in themselves, but for my faithful they represent a symbol. I need them found."

I did not know this Sheikh. I was curious to meet him. I asked Garbo about him. He had few. He only knew that he was a very rich man who had built a villa above the Dead Sea. He must have been powerful since that was a military zone not far from the border with Israel and from the archaeological park I was setting up. Garbo got in touch with the villa of the Sheikh, who invited me to breakfast for the following day and let me know that he would send for me.

Under the convent I had built a small parking lot. I waited there. The Sheikh's chauffeur arrived on time, greeted, ceremoniously invited me to take a seat in a luxurious black Mercedes. Everything from the off-the-shelf bodywork to the over-springing smelled of money. I wondered what the Sheikh looked like.

For a while we followed the road that led down to the Dead Sea. Then we turned left and climbed a hill. After about a kilometer the car took the turn a path that ran through two rows of trees bent by the wind, forming an asymmetrical dome. We stopped in front of an iron gate and the driver got out to open it. Then we went up a steep avenue which ended in front of a vast house whose architecture resembled that of a Swiss chalet. The trees in front of the house had been felled, so that I could see, on the slope below, a small village clustered around a white-domed mosque. Below, the Dead Sea, gray as that day.

The chauffeur opened the door. I got out and walked towards the front door. The door was opened by a friendly-looking woman who looked like a housekeeper and she was not an Arab. I entered a large vestibule. On one wall a long wooden coat hanger: instead of knobs I saw animal heads, there were lions, monkeys, cats and dogs. Men's hats and overcoats hung jumbled on some of those apples. Before me was a vast hall, the doors wide open. I saw absolutely nothing of Arabic and this amazed me. I could be in London, or in Paris, or in Florence, in a businessman's villa. To one side was a large fireplace. A log fire crackled behind the grate, the pine plank floor covered with kilim rugs. Everything looked neat and welcoming.

After smilingly assuring me that the Sheikh would come down at once, the housekeeper withdrew. I was about to sit down in one of the two armchairs in front of the fireplace when I heard blowing. A Persian cat stretched out on the cushion that covered the seat stared at me with hostile blue eyes. And another had immediately joined him. I looked at the cats who instantly arched their backs. I walked over to the fireplace as they both watched me closely. The logs slipped in a shower of sparks. A moment of silence followed. I assumed the Sheikh loved animals, but he didn't want to say anything. Many people loved animals and hated men.

The Sheikh appeared at the top of the stairs. The first thing that caught my attention was that the two Persians suddenly raised their heads, stared over his shoulders, then leaped lightly to the ground. The Sheikh had reached the foot of the stairs. He advanced on me with an outstretched hand, preparing to say a few words of apology.

"Forgive me, Father Matteo, I didn't hear the car coming."

"It was really kind of you to invite me to lunch," I said.

He was a tall man, about sixty, broad-shouldered, with straight, glossy black hair. Rosy cheeks, perfectly shaved, green eyes. He gave the impression of possessing considerable physical strength. He amazed me that he was sweating on his forehead and cheeks. He had a hairless face, a black veil on his lips, too light to hint at a mustache, too marked to reveal a bad beard. He was elegantly dressed. A blue jacket with gold buttons, gray trousers, a white shirt, a tie with a red background and small green designs, on his feet black Italian moccasins. He squeezed my hands vigorously.

"They look like steel," he observed.

"His too," I replied.

He smiled at me, looked carefully at his nails, showed them to me.

"I had them treated at the Intercontinental in Amman last night. There is excellent service, in every sense."

He winked at me. She seemed vulgar to me. Those pointy cut nails of hers glowed pink. She caught my gaze.

"They need to be covered in a light color to make them look good."

He smelled of a rather strong English cologne, on his right wrist he wore a solid gold bracelet.

"Have you made friends with Omar and Selim yet?" She pointed to the cats. "I'm convinced they can't stand the fact that I don't speak Persian."

He expected my laugh. I managed a smile and saw that he was pleased.

"Do you like cats?"

"Very. I had two when I was little."

"Omar and Selim have critical intelligence, I'm sure of it. You're not just any two cats, are you?"

He picked one up and showed it to me. She let go of him so that he was resting on the palms of her two joined hands. The cat then leapt to the ground and walked away with its tail erect. The Sheikh clapped his hands lightly together, as if to shake off the hair and dust.

"Beautiful, right? And so human. When the weather is bad they get nervous. Her cats were certainly intelligent too. I longed for some sun for his visit, Father Matteo. On a clear day, the view from here is quite beautiful."

"He must come to Nebo," I replied.

"We'll have a contest for the best view."

Then he said to me softly, with a slightly sinister chuckle: «I've learned in my life that, in addition to cats, you have to be familiar with waiters, croupiers, and beautiful women. So I'll call her hers."

I was dumbfounded.

"Do you like camels?"

I answered yes, with some astonishment. The conversation was taking a different turn than I had imagined. She told me she loved camels and had met many of them on her travels.

"Do you know Algiers?"

He didn't give me time to answer.

"In Algiers there is a casbah full of bad smells. After visiting it I decided that I would never go back to that city which had been the place of my dreams. Algiers first appeared to me in a pirate novel, in which the bey ordered a dreadful and funny torture. A complaisant horse carried a special saddle on its back and on the saddle a brazier with burning coals to which a poor man was tied. The horse rode around the casbah while the poor man's back was simmered. A camel would never accept that saddle. I especially love Mongolian camels. In summer they are slow and mangy. Only around the neck and on the sides do they have a few long, ringed tufts. In winter they are beautiful. Do you like tango?"

"Yup."

He sadly told me that he had suffered a lot from the

death of Atahualpa Yupanqui. He was eighty-three years old that great artist when he died in Nìmes. In Nìmes he had to participate in a festival and he had accompanied him.

"Death took him in his sleep. I was sleeping in a bed next to him and I didn't notice anything. Atahualpa was a guitar virtuoso and composed hundreds of songs and poems. He was a friend of Edith Piaf and it was he who made me love Carlos Gardel. Do you know the music of Carlos Gardel?"

I laughed.

"Why does he laugh?"

«Because Carlos Gardel el Rey is one of my favorite singers.»

He hugged me and told me that this really brought us together. It was amazing that I loved and knew Carlos Gardel el Rey. He was moved by intoning first Amurado then Sentimiento Gaucho with a gentle baritone voice and then he said: «Carlos Gardel el Rey was more beautiful and more elegant than me, he had many loves and when he sang everyone was moved. Carlos Gardel el Rey is a myth of my land that they forced me to leave. I come from an old family of officials. Scholars, engineers, officers and landowners. My great-grandfather was one of the four builders of Argentina's first railway. I was destined for a military career. I lost my estate due to inflation. I love my wretched country and I suffer because of that vulgar president. He is not a Peronist. Real Peronists, like me, have been kicked out of Argentina. I was little when Eva Peron died. General Perón was wise, he always smiled, and my friends and I considered him a genius. We had won an award with the school soccer team and the general dressed in white arrived on a Vespa to deliver it to us in person. He asked us if we had met Evita and with tears in her eyes he said that unfortunately Evita had died before seeing us as champions. Then the general turned to me, right to me, and he asked me: "And what do you want to be when you grow up, boy?". He asked us if we had met Evita and with tears in his eyes he said that unfortunately Evita had died before seeing us as champions. Then the general turned to me, right to me, and he asked me: "And what do you want to be when you grow up, boy?". He asked us if we had met Evita and with tears in his eyes he said that unfortunately Evita had died before seeing us as champions. Then the general turned to me, right to me, and he asked me: "And what do you want to be when you grow up, boy?".

"Peronist, sir general. What I have to offer you is fidelity together with a good character and courage".
The Sheikh was sobbing now, with an angry gesture he wiped away his tears.

"In my country, no one is an authentic Peronist anymore, do you understand? Everyone cheated. I wonder if Latin America really exists. I consider myself Latin American, and then Argentinean. Do you know our Indians? Good knights, good fighters, but lacking in imagination. I had an English grandmother who lived in Junin and met many Indians. I have always admired them and hated those who wanted to exterminate them. The Indians rode better than the gauchos, they didn't use spurs, they fought and died bravely, they used cruelty when they found it unavoidable. In the United States they called it the conquest of the West, in Argentina the conquest of the desert and it was a massacre. Today to purify my country we need the honor of the Indians, their seriousness, their loyalty. We Argentines love the boundless plains that resonate under the hooves of a horse. But it's a vanished world and even the tango is out of fashion. Does he know where he was born? In the brothels of Rosario and Buenos Aires with violins, flutes, pianos. It wasn't popular at first. Then, when ordinary people learned that the tango was danced in Paris, they accepted it. And the tango became respectable."

I was puzzled. Both the host and the welcome were completely different from what I had expected. There was something indefinable about him that came from the contrast between his appearance and his speech. Besides, it didn't take any effort of the imagination to picture him as a lover. Which, I reflected, suited a very few sixty-year-olds, and a few younger men too. I began to fantasize about his women. And I concluded with little originality: "It's pleasant to live here in the summer."

"Like at Nebo," he replied with equal banality.

He had opened a cabinet that stood next to the fireplace. "What are you drinking? Scotch whisky?"

"Yes thanks."

«Well, I prefer it to apéritifs too.»

He took a heavy crystal bottle and poured the liqueur into two long goblet glasses.

"Do you know that near your house is the place where John the Baptist baptized?" I told him.

"I've heard that."

«The Byzantine sources tell us that there was a priest who wanted to go to Sinai, the place where God had given the Law to Moses, passing through Arabia, that is, this territory of ours. Once crossing the Jordan, after a strong fever, he stops in a cave and in the cave he has a dream. An angel tells him: "Stay here, don't continue". The second night, the same thing. The third night too. Finally the angel says to him: "I am John the Baptist. You are going to Sinai, but here is the cave where I lived and where Jesus came to meet me and where I baptized

him". And there the monastery was built."
"I'm writing a book."
"His memoirs?
I saw him shake his head, a gleam of amusement in his eyes.
«No, Ayden melton. A Life of St. Francis."
He stared at me. He was convinced he had amazed me. I said seriously: 'It must be a considerable effort. I imagine he spoke to some of our friars. Or did he conduct his research in total autonomy? ».
He didn't answer me and replied: "I'm sure I'll die before I've finished it." She opened a bottle of wine.
"Aren't we drinking too much?"
«When the wine is good, it doesn't hurt. It's a picolit de Cormons that they bottle just for me." I drank. He was great. The thought obviously went to Garbo's wine. I grimaced.
"She does not like?" he asked worried.
"It's a wonderful wine."
"Why did he wince, then?"
"At Nebo we have a very modest wine." She relaxed.
«The advantage of St. Francis, from my point of view, is that so much has been written about him that I don't need to draw on sources for my material. I don't have to no research into the origins, you understand? The work thus achieves its purpose, allowing me to live here, practically idle, but with a clear conscience. At the first signs of boredom, I dive into my collection of works on St. Francis and write another thousand words for my book. When I've managed to convince myself of the usefulness of what I'm doing, I stop. As a pastime, however, I read scientific journals. I'm subscribed to the best ones.'
He raised his glass.

"To your health."

I offered him the opportunity to consult our archives. He replied: «But they concern the history of the Custody, not of Saint Francis».

"It is true."

"She will be my guardian angel."

"What do you mean?"

"As my first reader."

"All right." I sipped some wine.

"Do you know the purpose of my visit?"

"What makes you think so?"

I smiled, because I felt uncomfortable. I had the impression that I had lacked tact. She was looking at me thoughtfully and asked, "How would you react if I asked you an impertinent question? If I were to ask you, for example, to tell me sincerely if your interest in human weakness is one of the reasons for your presence in my house.'

I blushed. The meeting was moving in an unthinkable direction for me and I didn't like it.

"I assure you," I concluded, "that I am a very private person..."

He interrupted me slyly: "No offence, how much are your insurances worth?"

"I can give you my word that I would consider any information from you absolutely confidential."

"Oh yes?"

"Of course."

"Listen to me. Imagine this truth, the sky is black, the earth is blue, you do not meet angels and devils anywhere. Imagine that what I will tell you could happen and imagine that the time of wild days has come, in which everyone follows the strongest.

On the first day, Arafat unilaterally declares the

independence of Palestine. Israel annexes part of the occupied territories. Two Israeli soldiers are killed in a clash with Palestinian policemen. Prime Minister has Arafat's police barracks bombed.

On the second day, a car bomb explodes at the Tel Aviv train station, a suicide bomber blows himself up at a bus station in Jerusalem. There are dozens of victims, the prime minister orders heavy bombing. Two hundred Palestinians die, the majority are women and children.

On the third day, promising help to their Palestinian brothers, the Lebanese guerrillas of Hezbollah fired a volley of rockets at two Israeli kibbutzim in the Galilee. Israel bombs Hezbollah bases in Lebanon. The guerrillas react with long rockets ranged against Haifa and Tiberias. Israel bombs Beirut. Syria sends two divisions to Lebanon. A terrorist blows up a Tel Aviv cinema with all its spectators. Israeli helicopters attack the West Bank.

On the fourth day, Israel gives the Palestinians and the Arab countries twenty-four hours to restore calm: twelve Israeli fighter jets fly towards Beirut. Clashes intensify in the Occupied Territories.

On the fifth day, the radio broadcasts the coded message to call up the reservists. The prime minister declares a state of war. Israeli tanks attack Palestinian cities. Bands of Palestinians attack Jewish settlements. They are annihilated by helicopters.

On the sixth day, the Syrian president authorizes the artillery to bombard the Israeli positions on the Golan. Israeli Air Force destroys Syrian batteries. At the border there is battle between armored regiments of the two countries. Israeli paratroopers enter Syria. Israel evacuates settlements.

On the seventh day, a squadron of Syrian fighters

attacks northern Israel, which responds by bombing Damascus. Iraq launches ten Scud missiles at Israel. US naval aircraft in the gulf bomb Baghdad. Saudi Arabia and Kuwait ban their airspace to the US Air Force, which uses NATO bases in Turkey to strike Iraqi batteries.

On the eighth day more Scuds fall on Israel. Four Iraqi fighter jets violate Israeli airspace. Two are shot down, the others self-destruct against the skyscrapers of Tel Aviv. Israeli fighters bomb Baghdad, passing over Jordan which raises its fighters. They are all shot down. The King of Jordan sends his special forces to Ramallah and Nablus to protect the Palestinians.

On the ninth day, Egypt brings tanks into Sinai and then into Gaza. "I have no choice," says the Egyptian president. Israel bombs an Egyptian tank column. Syria launches a series of missiles against central Israel. Israeli fighter jets destroy the presidential palace in Damascus. Egyptian aircraft bomb the Israeli seaside resort of Eilat on the Red Sea. At ten in the evening, the news spread that Israel had aimed its long-range missiles, perhaps armed with unconventional warheads, on all Arab capitals. Half an hour later an Iraqi Scud with a chemical warhead explodes over Herzelya, a residential suburb of Tel Aviv. At midnight the United States orders a ceasefire within two hours: if it is not respected, they will go into action with all the means at their disposal.

On the tenth day the weapons fall silent before dawn. The war is over. In the following days Arafat and the Israeli prime minister meet in the White House, announce the resumption of negotiations "for the good of our children".

I was dumbfounded. She burst into laughter.

"Will you tell anyone about this possible scenario?" I

shook my head. She grinned.

«I'm afraid I haven't explained myself well, Father Matteo. The information itself doesn't matter. It's my position I worry about."

He paused, took the glass and emptied it all the way down. The housekeeper appeared and said he was ready. The Sheikh looked at me for a long time and asked me: "Do you ever think about the future?"

"Yup."

"Not me, he's coming too soon."

The dining room was oval. The table was lavishly set. A brocade tablecloth, Sèvres porcelain, crystal glasses, silver cutlery. We sat down. I to the right of him.

«As a scholar of human behavior, Father Matteo» he continued, «you will have noticed that generally, behind a person's actions, there is a stimulus that tends to dominate all the others. For some it is vanity. For others the satisfaction of the senses, for still others the desire for money and so on. I happen to be among those who have a highly developed love of money. But now let's talk about us. I guess you didn't come to see me to drink my picolit."

I was very explicit and direct.

"I'm told you've come into possession of two candlesticks."

"Did you know that cats get bored?"

"Are you bored too?"

«Bravo, Father Matteo, I was told that you are a very interesting person.» Then she frowned.

"I don't want to seem inappropriate, but I would like to know why you decided to come to me to recover the candlesticks."

"Monsignor Lahan."

"I see." Then, after a pause, he added, 'What I don't

understand is why so much importance is attached to two candlesticks. They are worthless on the market."
"I have no idea."

«Father Matteo, you want my confidences. The least she can do is reciprocate."

"It's the truth, I assure you. Besides," I added irritably, "I'm doing Monsignor Lahan a courtesy and that's it. But if those candlesticks are worthless, why are they in his hands?"
He poured more wine into the glasses.
"A toast to archeology."

I drank to please him. The wine choked him. To my surprise, I noticed that he was laughing.
"Excuse me, a sudden thought made me laugh."
"May I join in your entertainment?"
"In its time."

Still laughing, he patted me on the shoulder. She seemed suddenly in a great mood.

'My friend, please tell me you are not offended. Soon she goes to the table. I hope lunch is to your taste. Is she hungry? Greta, my housekeeper, is an amazing cook. After you, I'll solve the candelabra problem. Satisfied?"

"It's really nice of you to take so much trouble." She looked to me like she was about to laugh again, but she suddenly seemed to change her mind. On the contrary, she took on a very solemn tone.

«Don't even say it, Father Matteo. I like you, and it is rare for me to have guests in this house.' He hesitated.
"May I afford to give you some advice?"
"Of course."

"The advice is to enjoy the food."

We sat down at the table and ate Syrian rice made with yoghurt, roast chicken, aubergines stuffed with pine nuts and spices, roast mutton, various salads, including one made with chopped parsley and walnuts. We continued to drink picolit and, after a homemade ice cream, we were brought an aromatic coffee and a pear brandy.

My host explained that for a series of services rendered to King Hussein he had been appointed sheikh. He told me that, if things had gone the right way, today in his country he would have held a prestigious position.

"Instead he became a loyalist of the Hashemite monarchy."

«I collaborate with them when there are particular missions. And if you want to know more about me, remember that I love the game and women. I have different rules than you know. You should never leave your wallet or credit cards near me. But if you lost money to me playing poker, I think I'd use the money I stole from your wallet to pay you back."

"A little twisted."

"No, it's fair. And if I liked a woman particularly dear to her, I would make every possible attempt to seduce her and, having conquered her, I would cry with her all night and scream that that woman was a whore. »

"You forget that I'm a friar."

«Mine is a paradox. Come to the opera with me to see, for example, La Bohème. I will be moved. But if she offended my dignity, I'd be capable of killing her. Father Matteo, I'm a good person. Now I'm going to show you something that will really amaze you."

It was sunset when I left the Sheikh's villa. I had spent the whole afternoon in a dungeon filled with immensely valuable archaeological pieces. Behind a large velvet curtain was a flight of stairs. We went down a few steps, I found myself in a corridor with numbered doors on both sides. There was a smell that reminded me of a clinic. Each door corresponded to an archaeological area. The Capernaum gate offered my attention to a room that was already a museum in itself. I saw a veritable hoard of Byzantine coins. And the marble reproduction of the Ark of the Covenant. For him it was at the bottom of the Sea of Galilee.

The other gates were called Madaba, Macheron, Temple Mount, Mount of Olives, Nazareth, Bethlehem, Holy Sepulchre. It was as if that private museum, going beyond its current boundaries, drew a new map of places. When I arrived in front of the Nebo door I gave a start. I saw mosaics that I had been looking for for some time. They had probably been stolen before I became director of the archaeological mission. Or maybe later. I exclaimed: «But these mosaics are mine!».

He didn't answer me. She accompanied me, or perhaps pushed me, to the upper floor. The visit was over. In the hall he shook my hand and said: "The earth plays twenty-four hours a day, did you know that? Emits a continuous and modulated melody. But the man cannot hear her. It is many octaves lower than the perception possibilities of hearing. Do you think that by analogy Mars and Venus could also play. And who should conduct this space symphony? Don't you think it's a good question?'

I answered him thus: «Your question is a metaphysical one, I could tell you that God does nothing useless and that symphony is further proof of his perfection. That's why no one could direct it."
He smiled at me with great sympathy.

«Metaphysics, yes! In this regard, Father Matteo, what can you tell me about Carlino's collar?»

Father Luca had told me about Carlino, but not about his collar. What was the meaning of the Sheikh's question?

"I guess it's around the dog's neck," I said.

"Your chandeliers are waiting for you in my car," he said as he shook my hand.

CHAPTER SEVEN
VIDIGAL'S BIRTHDAY

That night at Nebo I had a long reflection. I had met Saul Bialik, I had seen Pascal Aretz die, I had saved Giulia Lazzari's life. The Keeper had enlisted me, the Sheikh was hiding many secrets. I found myself, unintentionally, at the center of a plot that I didn't control and in which, in addition to Bialik, the Sheikh and the Keeper, Carlino's collar also had its place. But what was the point? Could a dog's collar be worth anything? It was not an archaeological find. Or maybe yes?

I was rude to Garbo about the wine. He bought grapes at too high a price from the orthodox priest in Madaba. Using part of the money from offers and entrance fees.

If at the beginning the visitors were few and they were welcomed with sympathy and full availability, when the number increased, the sympathy remained, but for better hospitality it became necessary to build adequate structures and an investment was necessary. We were recovering part of that investment with the entrance ticket to the archaeological area and I could not accept that the orthodox priest of Madaba speculated on our money.

There were now hundreds of tourists arriving every day in both summer and winter. I had enlarged the square behind the church which had become a parking lot for coaches, and fenced off part of the archaeological area. Visitors walked along a tree-lined avenue, arrived behind the church, walked around it among a number of columns, bas-reliefs, funerary urns, and found themselves on the large terrace from which Moses saw the Promised Land.

My home and the guesthouse were under the church on the left. You had to go down a few steps, there was a small locked gate, and only Garbo and I had the key.

I treated him badly, therefore, I told him that his wine was vinegar and cost too much: while I was talking I knew I was being unfair. But the meeting with the Sheikh had irritated me. I apologized to him. We embraced. He promised me that he would discuss the price with the orthodox priest.

I went back to the other side, that's what Jordanians call the Occupied Territories, perhaps to give a sense of continuity to their country, since before 1966 the West Bank belonged to the Hashemite kingdom, and went to Bishop Lahan with the two candlesticks. Then I headed towards San Salvatore to meet the Custos. I introduced myself without being announced. I knocked on his study door and entered. I realized that I had taken him by surprise and this, for once, gave me some satisfaction. Without taking his eyes off the papers he was reading, he said, "He was right to come, I have to talk to you about a couple of things."

"I'm the one who has to talk to her."

"Oh yes?"

"Reverend Father, what do you know about Carlino's collar?"

«Carlino is Father Luca's dog. Why don't you go to Capernaum to see him? So you will also see Pug and the collar that apparently interests you so much.

"It's not just me."

"By the way, Father Sylvester has arrived in Cyprus and is well."

"I'm happy."

"I know you've made friends. I thought it would be better for Father Silvestro to spend a period of study and penance in Cyprus."

I asked him, "Have you ever heard of a man they call the Sheikh?" He grimaced.

«Tomorrow the Chapter begins. He's calm."

I greeted him. He made a gesture, as if to hold me back.

"Reverend Father, what is it?"

There was a pained expression on her face now.

"Do you want to tell me something about the Sheikh?" He didn't answer.

"Not feeling well?"

"I am fine thanks." I tried to insist.

"Do you need to tell me anything else?"

Result. He scratched his chin. The corner of his mouth trembled. It was unusual for him. She lowered her head to his papers again. I knew something was wrong, but I also knew that at the time he wasn't going to tell me about it.

I returned to the Flagellation full of doubts. I was worried. The atmosphere in Jerusalem was the same. There had been accidents, deaths, and as always the proportion favored the Cousins of the Wall. For four soldiers killed and three kidnapped by Hezbollah, there were more than thirty Friends of the Rock dead in the Territories, including many boys. And that pained me deeply. It was absurd to lose one's life like this. I thought that in Jerusalem they had always been used to living in an atmosphere of death. The city has seen and endured everything. Since the time of David and his son Solomon it has been burned several times, the walls torn down, its inhabitants torn to pieces and those pieces represent all the monotheistic religions. Death, in this sense, behaved democratically.

At the Flagellation I found many old friends. They had all arrived for the Chapter. I didn't see Luca and I imagined that he would arrive at the last moment. At lunch, in the refectory, I absentmindedly followed the conversation. I was in a bad mood, maybe I was tired. I slept for a couple of hours. It was unusual for me. I woke up even more nervous and more tired.

It was Father Vidigal's birthday. No one knew how old he was, or even if that was actually the day he was born. But he had decided so and had decided to celebrate it with me. I reread my translation of Domingo Badia y Leblich's Journey to Syria and Palestine. It seemed to me that I had well conveyed the sentiments and spirit of that Spaniard, spy of his government and scientist, who after having learned the Arab had perfectly traveled from Tangier to Constantinople under the name of Ali el Abbasi, convinced that different cultures could find common harmonies. It was my birthday present for Vidigal. He had come to visit me in the Studio dèlle Monete, he congratulated me on the conclusion of my work and suggested that I write an ideal sequel to Domingo Badia's book recounting my adventures in the Holy Land.

"Even the most secret ones. You have seen and heard things that many ignore. But if you decide to write it, don't talk about it with the Keeper. He would try to convince you otherwise, because, and I understand this, he is always afraid that events will be reported which, according to him, it is better to remain unknown. I, on the other hand, think that the more we talk about what is happening in the Holy Land, the better. And I suggest you some suggestive stories. Those on the Ark for example. I can help you. So, in the first part you will describe your adventures in the Holy Land. In the second part the stories of the Ark. I have a parchment in my archive that offers a possible but not shocking truth. I don't think anything shocking after the crucifixion of

Our Lord happened. The scroll is from a rabbi who lived in the late 1500s and early 1600s, Moshe Vinman. Moshe Vinman tells of the Babylonian invasion of the kingdom of Israel in 596, when Nebuchadnezzar's soldiers destroyed Solomon's Temple. According to Vinman, who was also an alchemist, the Ark would have remained in that area and he suggested digging on the al-Haram, between the al-Aqsa mosque and the Qubbet as-Sakhra mosque. A copy of the parchment came into the possession of the English archaeologist Oliver Carter - no relation to Tutankhamun's Carter - who secretly made an arrangement with the Turkish authorities. Oliver Carter began work near the great Stone from which, according to Islamic tradition, Muhammad on his horse Burak flew to heaven. Officially Carter was looking for the Well of Souls, but when the Palestinians realized that Carter was looking for something else, the English risked being lynched and the Christian community had many problems. The Keeper at the time was able to solve the case. Carter was repatriated and the excavation was closed. But there are other theories about the Ark. Some argue that it could be kept in a secret community of falascià, others in the basement of the Vatican. And then there's the matter of Carlino's collar."
"What do you know about Carlino's collar?"
«My memory is a good archive, unfortunately when I die the archive will be lost. There are secrets that a computer cannot keep, because the computer has no ethics. Pug's collar holds a big secret."
The tone was mildly ironic now.
«Do you remember, Matteo, when the Keeper told you, in his most serious tone, that our destination has us even if we don't know it yet? Instead, I beg you to always remember that the good earth belongs to those

who fertilize it. Like good books. But now we go down to our hosts.'

In the courtyard of the Flagellation there was a door that opened onto a somewhat damp room where provisions and other consumables were kept. I had transformed it into a warehouse, the repository for finds to be catalogued: pieces of mosaic still to be cleaned, fragments of Roman statues and other excavated objects.

On the long table where I used to work, two young friars had spread a paper tablecloth held in place by Roman heads and Byzantine feet. The glasses were of alabaster, I had found them in the tomb of an eighth-century merchant. The meat was cooking over the coals, there was plenty of salad and lots of fruit. The wine was that of Mount Nebo. Everyone liked it and I didn't comment.

Vidigal was moved.

«My friends, I will never tell you my age, but I have always been convinced of one thing: the brave are recognized more in small events than in big ones. I have based my life on this principle. And you, Matthew?"

The question amazed me. I wanted to ask him why he was addressing me, but I let it go. I spread my arms.

"Me too, of course."

«Matteo, in these parts everyone, even us Franciscans, were born in the midst of the blood of conflicts. Sometimes it seems that we would not even have an identity without an enemy in which to reflect the reasons for our existence. And in the leaders of both sides, when their prophecies of doom come true, one senses a sort of complacency. It is as if the Cousins of the Wall and the Friends of the Rock had accepted the aberration imposed on them by history, giving up wishing for a better future. Well, it must be said clearly that there is hope. What leaders don't do, ordinary people can do. It's the only alternative to the hate and despair we're getting used to."

We were all very attentive to Vidigal's words, which he continued.

"Now I will tell you the story of the Good Soldier."

"First," I said, "let's toast your birthday."

"But do you agree with what I said?"

"Yes," I said.

"Then I accept the toast."

We toasted and Vidigal recounted: «Imagine a neighborhood of East Jerusalem where the population is poor, hungry, the kids are scrawny. These verses are valid for them: "Here lie the dead because we did not choose to live and offend the land from which we were born. Losing your life is certainly not a great thing, but for young people it is. And we were young."

"Alfred Edward Housman!" I exclaimed.

"Well done Matthew. Imagine then that neighborhood where there are so many mouths to feed and the kids are armed with stones. The whitish peaks of the Judean hills are covered with a delicate green veil. On those hills young Palestinians lose their lives. In that neighborhood children offer their chests to an Israeli rifle inviting a teenage recruit to shoot. They live in miserable houses, where often the only piece of furniture, perhaps a cabinet with a glass display case, has been smashed during a search.

Imagine a child with one eye closed, yellow and full of pus. If you lift his eyelid you see that the eyeball is split. It's a rubber bullet that hit him. Imagine a stonecutter whose hand has been torn apart by a splinter. And, before arriving at the hospital, he was stopped at a military checkpoint and forced to kneel in the sun for hours. Imagine in what condition his hand is. Imagine a six-year-old boy hit in the face by a rifle butt for drawing the Palestinian flag on the wall. And another child injured all over his body by pieces of glass because a soldier broke through a window to get into his house. Imagine that all of them and others still are in the central and dusty street of their neighborhood, the one where the market is. An Israeli car arrives and the Good Soldier is driving. He is young. Maybe he doesn't realize where he's at. As soon as that people of cripples, mutilated, semi-blind notice him, they surround the car with him. The Good Soldier comes out, shoots in the air, flees. The car is burned and nothing more is known about the Good Soldier. Is the Good Soldier a coward, Matteo?»

"The answer is easy."

"Wait to talk," Vidigal said slyly. "Because the truth is always improbable. You will give a definitive answer in some time.

We ate and drank a lot. And the Nebo wine in the end didn't seem so bad anymore. After dinner Vidigal with his voice still ringing sang, accompanying himself on the guitar, some songs by Amalia Rodriguez. Shipwreck fascinated me, Trova do vento que pasa cheered me up, Madrugada de Alfama moved me. Vidigal spoke of his Lisbon, of the trams, of the dust and of the ancient atmospheres. And of a time that ended forever when Amalia died.

We went to sleep happy because Amalia had given unity to our emotions.

CHAPTER EIGHT
THE GIFT OF GENERAL MASSERA

"Have you ever thought about the power we have?"

Vidigal asked me as he left the meeting room in San Salvatore where the Extraordinary Chapter had taken place. I looked at him questioningly. The tone was mildly ironic. He went on: 'Think, my friend. It is one thing the one-hundredth of the power of the participant in a tribal assembly of a village of one hundred inhabitants, another the ten-thousandth of the power of a citizen of a Greco-Roman city-state of ten thousand inhabitants, yet another the fifty-millionth of the power of the anonymous voter of any democratic nation. I don't want to tell you that the Chapter is a tribal assembly, but the laity, improperly, could define it as a parliament in which we debate and appoint our ministers in a democratic spirit. And if so, think about it, we have power." He paused. "Until today. Because our Custos has transformed the Chapter into a brief board of directors» concluded Vidigal. «But he must have had his reasons. Still, I'm glad for you."

In fact, the Chapter had proceeded quickly and listlessly. There had been no preliminary meeting, let alone a discussion.

That was how it went. The Custos, who had seemed very tired to me, had celebrated mass, then we had moved into the meeting room, we had taken our seats, we had made the sign of the cross and the Custos, without a smile or a preamble, had told in a low voice: «Father Adelmo has returned, at his request, to Assisi. I ask you that Father Matteo be named in his place.'

Amidst murmurs of astonishment at the unusual procedure, the Guardian had added with a touch of irony I don't know how much voluntary: «I see and hear a unanimity of consensus and therefore from this moment Father Matteo is the Discreet who will represent the Italian linguistic community and he will take care of cultural affairs.'

Then, without saying goodbye to anyone, he left the room. Someone congratulated, not many to tell the truth, then Guillermo whispered in my ear that the Guardian was waiting for me in his private study. I found him sitting at his desk as usual. He asked me: «Happy?».

Without giving me time to answer, he continued: "Are you aware that torture is prohibited in principle by Article 5 of the Universal Declaration of Human Rights of 1948?"

I knew that he always started from afar to get to the substance of a matter.

He went on.

«Fanaticisms push the waves of the sea to the shore even when the wind has ceased. The most terrible torturers are actually small waves, greedy and corrupt bureaucrats, dedicated to theft and trade in the goods of the victims. They go to the torture cabinet every day as if it were their own office. They come home like any other employee and correct the children's homework, water the garden, go out in the evening to go at the cinema with his wife. Has he ever wondered how an ordinary man becomes a torturer? There is no passion. In most cases, a simple order is sufficient. And that guy obeys out of fear, cowardice, stupidity, lack of faith. There are other elements that contribute to the making of a torturer as well. For example, it's easier to become so if you've been mistreated. And torturing is certainly easier if you know that the victim belongs to the torturing class.

Many emotions passed on the Keeper's face, I had never seen him like this. It seemed that thousands of memories crowded inside him and disturbed him to the core. I realized that a part of his life had resurfaced. And he ran from his forehead to his lips with sudden pallors that told of long-held feelings and the memory of something or someone that at the same time gave him joy and suffering. His hands moved as if they belonged to someone else, they caressed his face, from which all traces of emotion and signs of memories of a distant time disappeared. For a moment there was no longer a wrinkle. I was privileged to see him as a young man. He said, "This morning I heard from a person I thought I'd erased from my memory."

Then he laughed and I saw for the first time that he had bad teeth. I understood how the indifferent air she often assumed stemmed from the fact that, knowing it, she kept her mouth shut as much as possible. I felt almost happy to know one of her secrets and figured she might have others and maybe I would find out the same way. The Guardian recounted: «When I met that person, he confessed to me that he had been a torturer. And he explained to me how he had become one. He had attended a boarding school based on the British method, which according to him taught a colonial mentality and imposed a very rigid discipline. Then he had believed all the state propaganda that he portrayed the guerrillas as communists who would ruin the country. Finally, during his military training, he himself had been tortured. Torture had concluded a course on evasion and escape. He and his companions had been captured, handcuffed, hooded and locked in a room. Every half hour the light came on and two soldiers watered them with jets of icy water. The next morning he had been dragged out of that room and forced to kneel on the concrete. The sharp stones cut his knees. A man asked him questions. He didn't know what to answer and so the man had pointed a rubber tube at his forehead and the frozen water had begun to flow on the hood that covered his face. The next morning he had been dragged out of that room and forced to kneel on the concrete. The sharp stones cut his knees. A man asked him questions. He didn't know what to answer and so the man had pointed a rubber tube at his forehead and the frozen water had begun to flow on the hood that covered his face. The next morning he had been dragged out of that room and forced to kneel on the concrete. The sharp stones cut his knees. A man asked him questions. He didn't know what to answer and so the man had pointed a rubber tube at his forehead and the frozen water had begun to flow on the hood that covered his face.

"You can hardly breathe," he explained. "The cloth gets into your mouth and nose and you get some air in, but not enough to survive. The feeling of being suffocated builds slowly, and you are afraid, even though you know it is a practice."

After training he joined a Marine corps set up to find guerrillas hiding in the countryside. When the tracks led to a small village in the wilderness, it was impossible to distinguish the footprints of the guerrillas from those of the locals. Then they chose a young man at random and asked him where the guerrillas had gone. If the prisoner claimed not to knowing this, he took a dynamo out of his backpack, attached an electric tweezer to the wretch's ears and turned the crank.

"Beating people or physically assaulting them was not part of our practice," he explained, "you need anger to do these things. It takes a particular mentality to take someone and beat them in cold blood." You have to consider it a profession and for him it was.

The Keeper paused. He was sweaty. He exclaimed, "How many years have passed!"

The corners of her lips slowly curled down. There was a glass in front of him. The fingers of his right hand moved quickly and grabbed him. He drank without realizing that he was empty. Then he showed me a newspaper page. I saw a picture of a man with a pleasant face. The Keeper hastened to tell me: "That face is deceiving."

He added: "It's former admiral Emilio Massera, a member of the Argentine military junta." Then he read: «Massera was arrested yesterday in Buenos Aires for the abduction of minors born to desaparecidos prisoners, a crime not covered by the Menem pardon. The admiral, who is now 73 years old, was placed in solitary confinement by judge Maria Romilda Servini de Cubria. Massera was in charge of the concentration and extermination camp of the Escuela Mecanica de la Armada. From there, the children born to the prisoners were given up for adoption to childless military families or to completely unaware couples. Considered one of the most ruthless and cruel leaders of the Argentine military dictatorship, the former admiral had already been sentenced to life imprisonment for three murders, twelve cases of torture, sixty-nine kidnappings and seven thefts. including precisely the abduction of minors from two couples of prisoners. After serving five years in prison, Emilio Massera enjoyed the pardon decreed by President Carlos Menem in December 1990».

"Did you know him?"

«Yes» said the Guardian, «at the time of the coup I was in Argentina. He's the man who explained to me what torture was."

He continued speaking in a low voice, but in such a way that I could hear perfectly.

«In Buenos Aires, in 1977, there is a military dictatorship. I'm on my way to see Admiral Massera. He looked for me. I woke up before dawn, with a sense of anguish. Though he's slept almost naked, I'm soaked in sweat. The acidity rises and falls like a column of mercury in my stomach. When I enter his office, the admiral is standing behind the desk. Smiling, he says to me: "Sit down, father".
He points me to an armchair. "A coffee? "
"Thank you. "

Massera gives instructions to one of his assistants so that no one interrupts us, and we are left alone, in an awkward silence. Massera breaks it off casually, while he spies on his every slightest gesture, trying to understand why he's been looking for me.

"How are you, father? "And without giving me the opportunity to answer, he says:" With the times that are running, the homeland requires total dedication from us. We didn't want the war we're fighting, they forced it on us. What's worse, they imposed it on a youth that could be valiant, that could still recover the values of the country if it stopped listening to the siren of the communists". He takes a short break. "We will win this war. I have no doubt. We are better prepared, we have the support of the people who want peace. Because the people always want peace, don't they, father?"

I don't know what to reply and he continues: "The people want to eat well, they want to go to the cinema, they want to dance the tango, they want to educate their children. Simple things, but that give flavor to life. We are forced to fight extremism, but I confess that I am a center extremist".
The admiral gets up and looks at the city through the

window.

"The problem is that we lack a new philosophy of life. Our men are worn out, our words are empty. We have to create something new. The people we fight have an ideal, but they are communists. I want the best of both sides. A nation is like a mosaic, each piece of the mosaic has a part of reason. "

The admiral approaches.

"We must take what is good in the Peronists, in the radicals, in the communists, in the conservatives. What do you think? "

Again I don't know what to answer.

"Our cause needs repentants, let me explain?"

Massera said this last sentence in a low voice, staring into my eyes. She then she tells me that those who do not repent are killed and their children given up for adoption. I react indignantly and tell him that I don't understand why he has sought me out. We greet each other coldly. The next day something happens that changes my life forever."

The Keeper paused for a long time. I asked him if he wanted some water. He stared at me, "Why?"

It was I who felt embarrassed. And before I articulated any answer, she recovered her alertness and presence, and her face returned impassive: "I haven't yet told you the reason for the meeting with Massera. I had a role of some importance in Argentina. It wasn't an official role, but let's say I was a sort of trustee of the Secretariat of State. And Massera knew it well. In his imagination there was the idea of using me as a privileged channel with the Holy See. Because he endorsed or at least he wasn't hostile to his project. The children of the desaparecidos would have been raised with regular adoption by those who had exterminated their family. The kids were never supposed to know who they really were who they considered their parents.

The next day, around midnight, a car arrived in front of my house. I had a house with two entrances. The secondary one, in the garden, overlooked a small road with little traffic. The house had been chosen by my predecessor, who was not a Franciscan but a Jesuit, and I had adapted to that situation, let's say, a bit too secular for me. My waitress came to call me visibly upset.

"There is someone in the garden."

I was in my studio and I was working. I went down to the garden and saw a young man in civilian clothes, clearly a soldier, who pointed to a bundle on the ground. Then he stood to attention, saluted me, and went out through the secondary door. I stood there, motionless with amazement."

I asked him the question he expected of me.

"What was in the bundle?" The Keeper shook his head.

«I want to tell you what was written on the note that the soldier had given me before leaving.» She recited in memory of her: "Father, have you ever wondered what order is? I did and I replied that the order is a matter of taste. The child I entrust to her charity is the son of two obstinate communists who are no longer on this earth and I don't think they dwell in our paradise. Father, open his arms wide, it's advice or maybe a prayer.

His friend Massera».

The Keeper spoke no more. He was absorbed in thoughts of him. Then he said to me: «Do you remember the story of the Good Soldier? Captain Shlomo Gillom who is surrounded by a group of Palestinians, abandons his car and his weapons and flees on foot with a limp, pursued by stones, while the Palestinians set fire to the car? A cold shower for the honor of Tsahal. Now he is accused of "cowardice in the face of the enemy", of "having betrayed his duties as a soldier" ».

The Keeper whispered as if following a thought of his: "Do you understand who the Good Soldier is?"

"Yes," I replied.

The Keeper was watching me intently now. And if he had told me all this it was because he trusted me. I felt that he was very tired. He trudged on.

"Shlomo grew up outside Argentina. He studied here. She will wonder why. Because this is a difficult and harsh country, and he's used to harshness. But also because I was transferred from Argentina to Jerusalem and I wanted him to live not far from me. »

"Did he feel like his father?"

The Keeper looked at me softly. But I quickly understood that the sweetness was reserved for Shlomo, not for me.

"There are many ways you can be a father."

Then, realizing he had said the obvious, he added: "But being good fathers is difficult."

He took one of his long breaks.

«Father Matteo, look for him, you will find him.»

It was almost an order. I returned to the Studium full of doubts. I undertook a job that concerned the church of Santo Stefano in Umm-er-Rasas, the ancient Kastron Mefaa of the Romans. I was trying to decipher a part of the mosaics that floored the church. There were sketches of vanished cities and I wanted to track them down. But I didn't know how. I had the scale reproduction of that mosaic and it was my evening pastime. I went to sleep with the Good Soldier problem. I didn't dream. When I woke up Rifaat handed me a note from the Keeper.

«Our dear father Luca died suddenly in Capernaum. Undeferrable commitments keep me in Jerusalem. You will give the funeral oration as a Discreet and will represent the two souls of the Custody at the funeral of our dear brother: the lay and the religious. A recommendation. Take care of Carlino, Luca was very fond of him. And when he returns to Jerusalem, remember to give me his collar. It will be a fond memory of the deceased brother."

CHAPTER NINE FUNERAL AT CAPHARNAUM

To the Custos of the Holy Land, Custody of the Holy Land,
Convent of St. Saviour, Jerusalem.

From Ayden melton,
Studium Biblicum Franciscanum, Convent of the Flagellation,
Via Dolorosa, 2nd Station, Jerusalem.

Reverend Father,
this is not a letter, but a report.

When I received your note with the news of Father Luca's death I suffered a lot also because you know very well what my relationship was with him. I had seen her recently and she seemed to be in excellent health. But the will of the Lord is wonderfully mysterious.

In the first place, I would like to tell you my funeral oration also because I represented you and it is right that you are aware of what I said.

The funeral oration was held in Capernaum in the octagonal church built on Peter's house. I imagine that you know it, although I don't remember if it was you who inaugurated it or someone sent from Rome. The large windows that open onto the Sea of Galilee have a certain charm, but that heavy glass floor that should allow pilgrims to admire the ancient stones on which Our Lord rested two thousand years ago is not a brilliant architectural invention. Because, through the crystal, the spiritual relationship that should be born between pilgrims and mystical stones freezes.

I began by recalling how Father Luca, the most

illustrious Franciscan archaeologist of his generation, had linked his name to the discovery of Peter's house in Capernaum.

«I was a pupil and friend of this man of great intelligence, strong passions and deep faith. When Luke reached the goal of his life, and found the house of the apostle Peter, I am convinced that he made peace with his harsh and merciless character. The holy place where, for some time, Jesus had lived and preached had been the great love of his earthly existence and, like any great love, full of moments of anger and sadness, violence and loneliness. Luca once told me, to explain the meaning of his work: "Read the Gospel of John and you won't find a word about Peter's house. Take the Gospel of Mark instead. He insists on this all the time and do you know why? Is simple. Mark wrote his Gospel in Rome under the influence of Peter. Did Peter perhaps want to glorify himself? Not at all.
Christian not so much because it was his home, but because it was the house where Jesus had slept".

Reverend Father, I assure you that everyone was moved at this point. I was right to quote Luca's words exactly. I continued in a more conversational tone:
"This place was home until the fifth century, when they built a church on it. There is a continuity of life here that is not found in Nazareth or even in Jerusalem, and this always amazed Luke. And he explained to me how it was the only house in Capernaum to have become a meeting place for the Judeo-Christian community. Digging he discovered how the central octagon had been built exactly on the perimeter of a quadrangular house. The pilgrim Eteria had seen, and she had left written about it, a house transformed into a church, and that house, the faithful of the place had told her, was Peter's house which you can now see below ».

At this point, Reverend Father, I paused for a long time, let's say it was a voluntary quotation from the pauses you make. I changed my tone: «Friends, I realize that I have told you something that many of you already knew. It seemed to me the best way to remember our friend. In fact, I have the feeling that he spoke to you through my mouth. Now I want to show you the place where Luca has been resting since yesterday."

We left the church. Luca's friends, about twenty, followed me. We went down a few steps. To the right, in a flowerbed, his grave. On the black stone tombstone this inscription:

«Not everything, once your life is over, will leave with you».

One thing surprised me and I questioned Omar, the Palestinian handyman who supervised the small convent, cooked, cleaned, a bit like Garbo al Nebo. I was curious to know how he managed to order and have the tombstone in two days. Omar explained to me that Luca had had it prepared for two weeks, as if he knew he was about to die. This surprised me a lot. So when we dined together in the refectory of the Flagellation, Luca had already ordered the tombstone, but he didn't exactly look sick.

I was attracted by a beautiful, young, blonde woman who was holding a little girl of about five, brown hair long and straight to her shoulders, blue eyes. The little girl, smiling, approached: «What is your name?».

"Matteo."

"And you?"

"Sylvie. And that"—the blond woman pointed to me—"is my mother Annie."

"She looks like your sister," I said admiringly.

I assure you, Reverend Father, she was quite a beautiful woman. The little girl said to me, pleased:

"Everyone says so."
"Did you know Luke?"
"My mother studied with him."
Annie came over: "My daughter is a chatterbox."
"It is very nice. She told me that she studied with Luca. »
"Yup. He was a great friend and a great teacher to me."

The tone struck me as somewhat rhetorical. Annie looked tenderly at Luca's grave. She then took Sylvie by the hand and walked towards the convent. I followed her because I too was going in the same direction.

I must tell you, Reverend Father, that the small convent requires a strong restoration. Strange that Luca had never told me about it. I noticed that Annie was following my movements out of the corner of my eye. I joined her and said: "I too am a guest of Omar."

She looked relieved. The others were leaving. Annie said something to a tall man whose face I couldn't see because her back was to me. She noticed, she had an expression of annoyance. We entered the house. A long corridor and on the left a large room with a television. Annie said proudly that it was she who had given Luca the satellite dish and he was happy to see the world in the evening.

«Luca cultivated a dream. Him digging in Yemen, looking for the treasure of the Queen of Sheba. But he also wanted to find the Ark of the Covenant. And discover the true places of Sindbad."

I thought maybe we knew two different Lucas. We were sitting on an old flowered sofa. The worn tile floor, the white walls with some cracks, everything smelled clean. A dachshund yelped, ran back and forth, calmed down in Sylvie's arms.

"Carlino is sad about Luca's death," said Sylvie. «He seems to have lost his mind. At times he thinks that Luca is still alive and hiding somewhere. So he goes looking for it." Carlino was now licking Sylvie's nose, then her hands and she licked his nose too and Carlino moaned with pleasure. I went to the bathroom. The dog followed me, growled, put his muzzle on my feet as I washed my face and hands. I remembered that it was Luca's bathroom and thought maybe I was the first person to use it after his death. I went back to the room, Sylvie took Carlino in her arms again and caressed him. The dachshund yelped and jumped out the window. Annie said, "He does that often."

We entered an old, large kitchen, two windows overlooking the Sea of Galilee, a door that opened onto the outside, a rectangular table set with a tablecloth with green and light blue squares, paper napkins, tin cutlery, white and scratched by use.

"I cooked it," Annie said. «Pasta with sauce, Milanese cutlets, roasted potatoes as a side dish. She likes them?". I was realizing that Annie was at home.
"I'm glad to finally meet you." She told me. "Luca always talked about her." I didn't know what to answer and drank a glass of wine in one gulp.

"It's the wine Luca liked," Annie said, "it comes from a vineyard a little to the south. I believe that a sincere friend, with whom you share everything, is irreplaceable. In our work the relationship between faith and archaeological discovery is close and if suddenly the friend you worked with is no longer there, the day becomes very sad.»
The words broke in her throat.

"Last month I was here for a few days. One night I hear Pug barking. I leave my room and see him at the bottom of the stairs licking Luca's face. He had passed out. He had in his hand his favorite work tool of his, the trowel, that one of bricklayers. Luca used it in the final phase of the excavation, when his sensitivity warned him that he was about to find something important. I helped him back to bed."

He changed his tone. He called, "Carlino, Carlino." The tone was concerned.

"Where are you? You don't have to walk away. Are you offended with me? Father Matteo, I also buried Luca's few clothes. Maybe Carlino is sorry he can't smell them anymore.'

He was shouting now: "Carlino, where are you?"

The phone rang. Annie jumped up and ran into the corridor, where there was an old black telephone plugged into the wall. I heard her speaking softly and in Hebrew, but I couldn't understand what she was saying. Her face darkened again and she looked at Sylvie. She then she shook her head as if to dismiss bad thoughts of her. I asked her more and more perplexed:

"Problems?".

Sylvie came to her mother's rescue.

«Do you know that Luca baptized me?»

"Go to bed, it's late," Annie said dryly.

"Can I take Pug with me?"

"If he comes back, sure."

"It's his mother who gave Carlino to Luca," she told me.

The dachshund came back through the window and curled up next to Sylvie. Annie gave me a worried look. Sylvie went up to the bedroom with Carlino in her arms, who was whimpering as if he were in pain. Annie's manner puzzled me. The things she had told me didn't convince me. She asked me, "Don't you feel like someone is watching us?"

Without giving me time to answer, with a half smile on his mouth, he bade me good night. I wasn't sleepy. I went out, near Luca's tomb I instinctively made the sign of the cross. Out on the water, about a hundred yards away, I noticed a motorboat. It seemed to me that someone from the boat was making signals with a flashlight. I turned myself. Behind me, from the old synagogue, they responded with a smaller beam of light. "It's weird, isn't it?"

Annie's voice made me jump. I turned myself. But it was already gone. That woman moved like a cat or like a ghost. I thought I saw her at the old synagogue and a shadow next to her. I heard shots coming from the lake. A lookout headed for the motorboat. She then she screams in pain. The speedboat was being pursued by her lookout and machine guns. Suddenly everything calmed down. I quickly returned to the convent. I fell asleep in Luca's study thinking about the fight and Annie's behavior. I was woken up by someone banging on the door. I opened. Sylvie was sobbing.

"Carlino is missing. This night he wanted to leave my room. He was agitated.

I couldn't find it this morning."

Annie came up. Her face was very placid. She said she wanted to talk to me.

We strolled to the shore.

"Someone is watching us."

I told her they were watching her. There was no reason for anyone to care about me.

"There are always reasons."

He walked towards a group of pilgrims. I returned to the convent. Annie joined me shortly after, worried.

"Did you meet Sylvie by any chance?"

"No."

"She left without telling me where she was going."

He angrily stamped his right foot on the ground, grit his teeth, entered the house. I followed her, I wanted her to explain the shooting at night, the disappearance of Carlino and then of Sylvie.

The phone rang. This time I was quicker than her, I replied. On the other side a familiar voice.

"I'm Bialik, I need to talk to you. He will find a car outside the archaeological area. »

The driver was the usual silent soldier who never smiled. On the road full of evangelical memories that skirted the Sea of Galilee up to Tiberias, I tried to reflect. There were too many elements that I missed. Reverend Father, as they say, the skein became more and more entangled. Bialik was waiting for me sitting at a table in a cafe in the center of Tiberias.

"Bialik, please tell me, did you come on a trip to the Sea of Galilee?"

He was about to answer me, but preferred to bite into a sandwich. A drop of mayonnaise fell on her shirt.

"Do you want some water?"

He shrugged and used a handkerchief to disastrous effect.

"We call this lake Kinneret, and do you know why? We have compared it to a lyre, the Kinnor. This means being pragmatic!» she exclaimed with deep satisfaction. He sighed for a long time and asked me, "What about Annie?"

"That he has a lovely daughter, Sylvie, and Sylvie is missing."

"Now she's back."

"Did you have her kidnapped?"

"I don't kidnap little girls."

"And not even dogs?"

"No." He answered curtly. And she added, "I'm wondering if you are protecting Mrs. Annie for some reason or if you are her accomplice."

"An accomplice to what?"

"About the terrorist action last night. I guess he noticed that. Or was she asleep? No, I don't think he was asleep. He walked like a tourist on the shores of the lake, while a small war was taking place a few meters away. »

«Bialik, you are free not to believe it, but I was thinking of my friend Luca.»

"It seems he was a great archaeologist."

"Indeed."

"And you didn't realize that a band of Palestinians was trying to disembark? Luckily we were able to intercept them. His friend Annie was waiting for them to give them the map of the power plant they were going to blow up."

"Bialik, they sound like fantasies to me."

"No. There's a power station around here and we thought it was the only possible target. And his friend Annie is part of the gang."

"The evidence?"

"My intuition."

"So you have no proof."

"Not necessary with terrorists."

"Bialik, I want to know who Annie is."

"Ask the gang."

He laughed and added, "The trouble is, they're all dead."

"How many were there?"

"Three."

"And Annie would be the fourth element for you?"

"The fourth or fifth."

"And where is the other one?"

"I do not know."

"Bialik, Mrs. Annie Deroche is a student of Luca's, and now lives and teaches at the University of Amman."

"I don't know. And by the way, if that were the case,

she could teach college and be a terrorist, one thing doesn't exclude the other. Do you think so?"

"What do you want from me?"

«Look at what has been happening in recent weeks. Thirty parties or an electoral system based on a senseless proportional law are not enough. Now small groups of religious fanatics, financed by American Jews, are also setting about organizing Terror against Terror, as they call it, with crazy plans for retaliation against the Palestinians. The truth is that as soon as we come into contact with the state and with power, we get the urge to mix with metaphysics, with morals, with religion. After all, you expect this from a people like ours, so ancient and quarrelsome. We are capable of destroying our state. It has already happened in biblical times. A group of Jewish terrorists, some time ago, wanted to blow up the Al-Aqsa mosque. Rabbi Kahane's followers want to provoke holy war, unleash hordes of furious Arabs against Israel to see if God exists, if God is really with us. Using the state to settle one's accounts with the Almighty and quench one's thirst for the sacred. Father Matteo, tell me in which other country in the world something like this could happen. We don't have an army, but a Crusader cavalry. Elsewhere there are the infantry, the engineers, the navy, the air force. Here our people have to be heroes even when they don't feel like it. Take the case of the Good Soldier. He didn't have to flee in front of a couple of young Palestinians armed with stones. He had a moral obligation to use weapons and, if it was unavoidable, to kill. Believe me, there is nothing to understand. We are a population of about five million inhabitants who crowd into a territory less large than your Sicily.

With the old borders before 1967, the only ones still internationally recognized today, eighteen kilometers separated Jordan from Tel Aviv, thirty-five from Haifa, thirty-six from Ashdod. How long does it take for a jet to travel thirty-five kilometers? And how many minutes does it take for a tank regiment to swallow eighteen kilometers? Here, for thirty-five years, everything has always played out in a few hundred meters that made the difference between life and death, along a border that ran between the houses, in front of a balcony or a garden.»

He took a breath, changed his tone. He was less excited now.

"Father Matteo, I cannot arrest Annie Deroche in a place that belongs to you Franciscans. The Keeper wouldn't forgive me. You must do me the courtesy of leading her off your property. Because, if you have followed my speech, you will have understood that I cannot behave otherwise. »

"Do you want to arrest the child too?"

Bialik did not answer me. I told him I would think about his request. I found Sylvie smiling. She had gone for a walk on the lake shore to reflect, she explained to me in a serious tone. She alone. We had worried unnecessarily. She hugged me. Annie told me they were leaving very early the next morning.

"It's quieter in Amman."

I told her I had to talk to her. She changed expression.

"Sylvie, go find Carlino."

Sylvie, walking away, looked at me knowingly.

"Annie, you risk going to prison. And the prisons here are very harsh, especially for terrorists."

He shook his head.

"It's ridiculous."

"A certain Bialik wants to arrest you."

«Father Matteo, I am going through a crisis with my husband.»

"Is your husband not in Jordan?"

"My husband is here. And the man he saw me talking to after Luca's funeral. He is a doctor and moves to London. He wants to take Sylvie away. Sylvie was with him when she disappeared. They talked for a long time. Sylvie has chosen to stay with me. It's the truth, terrorism has nothing to do with it. However, if you want to know more, I can tell you that I'm working on a book and I walk alone at night to concentrate."

I told her that she had convinced me. I tried to explain it to Bialik.

«Bialik, you build up an idea of a person and you can't move from that idea. Her ideas are boulders."

"Boulders that allow me to do my job well."

"And the irony, Bialik?"

"What does it mean?"

«Irony is also flexibility.»

"What does irony and suppleness have to do with Annie?"

I was amazed that he hadn't called her Madame Deroche again.

«Bialik, for me flexibility and irony are not a gesture of superiority, but a form of life. To her they represent the enemy.”

And then I did something I had read in a spy book. I told Bialik that we would meet at a certain time outside the convent. And I didn't want to see any of his folks around before then. Bialik accepted. I timed it right, Annie and Sylvie had a three-hour head start. They crossed the border without problems. Annie called to thank me and recommended that I take care of Carlino.

She would come back for him when the situation allowed.

When I met Bialik, he immediately understood that I had deceived him. He told me the words I imagined. Because of my levity Tsomet had suffered a defeat. There had been a chance to capture Annie Deroche, the protagonist of many terrorist acts, but I had helped her escape. I calmly replied that Annie Deroche was a simple university lecturer and he had only done a good deed by allowing her to return undisturbed to Amman with her daughter.

Bialik didn't doubt my good faith, but he found me too humane and open to dialogue. Terrorists are terrorists, and even though he considered me one of the few capable of dealing with everyone, that didn't mean I could decide on my own. I suffered his assault in silence convinced that he was up to something, otherwise he wouldn't have insisted so much on Annie Deroche's danger.

Reverend Father, I may have been wrong in helping her to leave, but no one could convince me that Annie had suddenly become dangerous.

"Our current situation is bizarre," said Bialik, "for example, we cannot understand whether the Syrians are really willing to recognize the legitimacy of our existence. As for the Palestinians, I have the feeling that for the first time in their history they accept the idea that we exist. The negotiation will be long. For definitive peace it will take time, patience, good will. There is an idea that runs through the heads and hearts of some of us. Jordan is an invention of the British. They brought together some Bedouin tribes under a king who arrived in Mecca. Today, the majority of Jordan's population is made up of Palestinians. And those who live in Israel, if they don't want to accept our rules, could move en masse to Jordan. We have to defend our security. Annie works for terrorists and pretends she doesn't remember the Holocaust. She believes in hate and destruction."

"And you, Bialik, believe in propaganda."

Bialik changed his expression and brought his face closer to mine.

"We must fight terrorism and at the same time travel the paths of peace. I know you are a sincere man. You sometimes rude, but sincere. »

He touched my arm. I pulled away almost in revulsion. Something happened that amazed me. Bialik smiled at me, long, sympathetically. He grabbed my right hand and squeezed it warmly. I was baffled. Bialik bent his head over his left shoulder, until his ear touched the humerus. He said to me: «Father Matteo, you attended a play where Annie was mirrored, but the mirror reflected another image».

He offered to go back with him in the car. We spoke no more until Jerusalem. The road that passed through the occupied territories and Israeli settler settlements it seemed to me, Reverend Father, hostile. It was the first time I had this feeling. We arrived at the Talmudic Institute with a strong sense of mutual unfamiliarity. Bialik asked me where I wanted to be taken. I answered curtly, "Nowhere."

The last thing I have to tell you, Reverend Father, is that when I left, Carlino had disappeared again. By the way, Reverend Father, Carlino had no collar.

CHAPTER TEN SAN'A

To the Custos of the Holy Land, Custody of the Holy Land,
Convent of St. Saviour, Jerusalem.

From Ayden melton,
Studium Biblicum Franciscanum, Convent of the Flagellation,
Via Dolorosa, 2nd Station, Jerusalem.

Reverend Father, I continue my report.

When my soul is troubled and I have to reflect, I usually walk. From Agron Street I walked up to the King David. Then I entered the Pontifical Biblical Institute of the Jesuits. I stopped for a few minutes in the library. Think, Reverend Father, it contains more than six thousand volumes of archeology, especially biblical. When I left, I met a driver I knew, an Israeli. He had to go to Allenby Bridge to pick up some French tourists arriving from Jordan and I took advantage of his courtesy. All the way down he spoke with intense concern about Palestinian aggression. A cousin of his had been killed near Ramallah. He was a settler. I tried to explain to him that a few hours earlier the Israelis had killed four Palestinians, two of whom were under fifteen. But, Reverend Father, he didn't even listen to me. He kept repeating obsessively that all Palestinians are murderers. There was little traffic and we quickly arrived, to my great relief, at Allenby Bridge. And there a funny and telling thing happened. The fat soldier from the slap was on duty at the border post where they examine passports. He was eating some pasta like last time. He recognized me and a fearful expression came over his face. I understood that it wasn't the fear of another slap that made him nervous, but the fact that I might again spill his precious plate of pasta on his head. Then I smiled at him and nodded a blessing. He was so scared that he forgot he was Jewish and closing his eyes made a very quick sign of the cross. Maybe he thought it was the price to save pasta.

I had phoned Garbo to come get me and great was my astonishment to see the Sheikh's chauffeur instead. I thought he was there for someone else. Instead he came up to me and he told me the Sheikh was waiting for me. I replied that I had no appointment with his master. He replied that I had better follow him. The threat was so ridiculous that I laughed. I got into the car more amused than annoyed. But when I realized that the car was heading for the airport and not the Nebo, my amusement turned to amazement. Which increased when, near the airport, the vehicle took a dirt road that led us directly onto a secondary runway. There was a small jet. And standing in front of the open hatch, the Sheikh was waiting for me with a big smile on his lips. He said, "I thought you might like a ride on my new toy." Then, changing his tone and feigning concern: «But do you like flying?».

Reverend Father, the walk took me to Yemen, to San'a. In that old and dirty airport the Sheikh handed out handshakes, pats on the back and many dollars to the border guards. Nobody asked me for my passport, which I obviously didn't have. I forgot, Reverend Father, part of the trip was dedicated to listening to the songs of Carlos Gardel. The Sheikh stuck a cap on my head, he had one too, and for three hours he moaned, he was moved, he patted me on the back. Then he bit into some sandwiches with chicken and mayonnaise – I didn't want anything because I hate eating between meals –, he drank a beer and fell asleep.

The arrival hall was also the departure hall. It was long and narrow. It looked more like a train station than an international airport. Very thin men dressed in the same shabby way walked up and down it. A gray and threadbare jacket, a colorful floor-length skirt, a sash around the waist, in the sash a dagger, the jambiya. I saw daggers with large, precious handles and shiny, sharp blades. They shone, and the contrast with the poverty of the place seemed sharp and strong.

I saw no women. The crowd of armed men stopped every now and then, took something green out of a plastic bag, put it in their mouths and chewed with determination and pleasure. Then someone lay down and others placed themselves next to him and a ragged, dirty, silent pile was formed. I saw only the mouths moving, deformed by a kind of ball that got bigger and bigger. I assumed it was due to that green food.

The Sheikh told me that green food was called qat, Yemenis often chewed it, drawing strength from it. I asked him if he had tried it. He replied that he had chewed it on a previous trip to San'a, but he hadn't offered him any particular emotions. A black Mercedes was waiting for us. The driver's name was Nabil, he had a long and precious dagger. The Sheikh admired the quality of the handle and Nabil explained how the jambiya had belonged to his grandfather's grandfather and an American had offered him five thousand dollars, but he had refused. The symbol of her family and his history was not for sale, he said proudly. The jambiya, the Sheikh explained to me, represented myth, memory, the present, honor, tradition, accompanied the Yemeni from birth to death and was handed over from father to son.

I could not see well the road that led to San'a. In any case, it seemed to me that I was traveling in the middle of the sky. The hotel, near Al Tahir Square, appeared to me modern, comfortable and empty. The Sheikh warned me that Nabil would be our guide and bodyguard. It was at that point that I asked him what we had gone to San'a to do. He replied that he was tired and would explain it to me the next morning.

I understand, Reverend Father, that you might ask me why I didn't ask that question earlier. The answer is simple and if you allow me quite obvious. The story of Capernaum had touched my heart. I was in pain and wanted to isolate myself. And since providence exists and if we don't believe it, Reverend Father, who can believe it, I had welcomed the invitation of a bizarre character like the Sheikh to take a walk in the Middle Ages.

I slept in a small, perfumed room with bamboo furniture. The Sheikh made me find pajamas on an armchair; and clothes of my size, and, in the bathroom, a toothbrush, toothpaste, razor.

Early the next morning I went down to breakfast and found a note from him. He had gone out early to do a certain thing that might interest me too. Nabil was at my disposal and he was waiting for me. He told me that he would show me the Old City and asked me if I had ever seen a thief punished. I answered no and he told me that just a few days earlier, in the large Al Tahir square, a thief had had his left hand cut off and, he added admiringly, had not uttered a moan. The cut of the hand, Nabil considered useful and educational. It meant that the thief had been punished and that from now on he would behave himself. It was in a sense a certificate of guarantee, he explained to me. We went to visit the qat market.

"The qat around here," Nabil told me, "isn't the best. The best is in the mountains, in Shahara. You need love for your qat, it's not easy to find."

The market began on the road and continued between alleys and old houses. I saw many trucks stopped, as if they had been suddenly abandoned. The qat was wrapped in banana leaves and around the vendor, who touched his bunches as if they were treasure, many people argued. I followed Nabil, but at a distance, because I understood that he didn't like being around him. The bargaining was violent, I didn't understand if they were arguing about price or quality. Probably on both. An old man, after a quarrel with a buyer, while he was turning away from him, took one of his decks and threw it at him with rage and violence. The man hit on the head turned, grabbed his jambiya, then grimaced, walked away. Nabil told me, "I don't feel love here. There is no good qat.'
I asked him how he recognized good qat.

'Good qat,' he explained, 'is what one really feels. It takes love between the qat and whoever has to chew it. My qat must rustle between my fingers and I must hear it as I hear the sea in the shell. The qat is a friend with whom you spend a few hours of the day alone. Alone, because, even if you consume him in the mafray with the other men, in reality you are alone with him.'

I asked him if there were days when there was no love and he ran out of qat. He replied that it never happened. Also because, he said proudly, he could spend and love often depended on money. The poor ate the larger leaves and the rich the smaller and more tender leaves.

Finally Nabil found his qat. He sniffed the leaves, rubbed them gently on his face, sealed them in a plastic bag which he slipped into a jacket pocket. He was calmer now, and he told me that in ancient times there were many gates in San'a, eight, maybe ten, which were opened when the sun rose and closed when it died. But for foreigners there was only one gateway, because an ancient prophecy said that a foreigner would have caused the ruin of the city.

So the stranger who arrived in front of that door pulled a string and the string rang a bell and the guardian asked who he was and what he wanted and the stranger answered and, if the answers were satisfactory, only at that point was the door opened and the foreigner could enter the city. Many centuries had passed and the only door that remained intact was precisely that of the foreigners, the Bab al Yemen door.

In front of the Bab al Yemen gate I heard the music of the jambiya dance for the first time. At first it all seemed the same to me, made of hard-beaten drums. Then I heard a melody devoid of sweetness, something barbaric and ancient that expressed a strength based on the swiftness of the dagger and the agility of the horse. Nabil invited me to enter a Turkish bath. A voluptuous melancholy invaded me while, lying down in a dark room, I smoked a hookah thinking of so many distant things and the masseurs rubbed and dried me. Then I felt suffocated in the damp room air. I went out and the city appeared to me very white, miserable, haughty. There were many beggars in front of the Bab al Yemen gate. I saw a man dragging a deformed and monstrous foot, a gray loaf of bread from which motionless appendages were protruding. The man advanced on two crutches begging for alms. Another beggar was crouched in a cart and a child was pushing the cart back and forth, some on the sidewalk, some on the road between the dust and stones. The man in the cart was moaning softly, evenly and monotonously. It seemed to me that someone, with precise determination, had broken his bones at every point.

Whoever passed by and took pity threw coins on that ragged human heap and the child thanked him by shouting: «Allah is great, Allah is great».

I gave the boy some coins. With a cold, careful look he counted them and with a half smile of satisfaction he pocketed them. Another boy tugged at my jacket sleeve. I went to offer him some money but he shook his head. He wanted me to follow him.

I saw in his eyes a request that was not desperate, but strong. We took a few steps. Behind a counter where they sold seeds and hazelnuts, I saw a very thin old man lying on dirty sheets of newspaper. The old man was barely breathing. Still looking at me, the boy squeezed my hand.

We got closer, I realized that the old man was dying. The boy took the old man's hand and mine. The old man died and the boy looked at him in wonder. I offered him money again, and again he didn't want it. He stroked my face softly and walked away. Nabil was frowning at me. I understood that he was disapproving of me.

Beyond the Bab al Yemen gate was a busy square and souk. The smells mixed together, with a strong prevalence of cinnamon. I saw many camels, old and wrinkled. On the ground the gravel mixed with the dust. The dominant color was gray.

The souk was made up of small shops one and a half meters above the ground. I found gold coins, Maria Theresa thalers, matches, tins of sardines, shoe polish, cheese, rice, coffee, tea, copper dishes, potatoes, soaps, sandals made from car tires.

Nabil led me to a low, wide inn. There was an oven that looked like a well and a cook kneaded and threw the dough that stuck to the walls into the well. When it was cooked the cook took it out and wrapped it in loaves of many shapes. The cook opened the belly of a large fish, removed the spines and quickly painted the meat with a thick and fragrant sauce and it turned reddish. The big fish went to the bottom of the well.

The inn had wooden planks that were not very clean. Nabil caught my eye and with a smile he took some paper and scrubbed the table. But the dirt had ancient colored crusts and little red, alive animals. Nabil shrugged as if to tell me that he had done what he could.

The cook took the well-cooked fish out of the well and placed it in a large metal dish. On another plate the bread was rolled up, with its puffs and lace. Nabil looked at me happy, put his finger in the fish's eye, picked it up with his fingernail, sucked it and told me it was delicious. He took the other eye and offered it to me. I refused. He sucked it with pleasure. The meat was soft and aromatic, the bread soft. We ate our fill.

I returned to the hotel very tired. I went up to my room. I took a hot bath. I lay down on the bed. Without knocking the Sheikh entered with a big smile and a bottle of cognac under his arm.

"It's contraband. In these parts they are Shiites and very fundamentalist. Father Matteo, would you like a sip?» I toasted with him to I don't know what. He said, "What I'm looking for is no longer in San'a. Let's go to Taizz.'

The next morning we left early. Nabil was driving and the Sheikh quickly fell asleep. The road to the South was discreet and above all paved. I had the feeling that Yemen was a place on the edge of the world, from which one could fall at any moment.

Nabil told me that once upon a time that land was rich in incense and the incense stuck to the beard of the goats. In front of each town we passed through I saw a kind of triumphal arch adorned with photos of the Yemeni president in civilian clothes and uniform, two eagles on the inverted crescent, the Koran open with two arrows facing each other. Underneath were some floral decorations and grapes.

We met many checkpoints, Nabil showed the soldiers a card. He explained to me that it was a pass with our names on it. So, he smiled at me, the government could always know where we were. I remarked that they should have checked our passports as well to see if the names on the paper matched. He said that in a way I was right and he didn't speak to me again for some time, as if my remark had irritated him. We passed by some qat plantations. Nabil greeted the green plants with affection and deference. He told me that the qat there was of good quality. He could have stopped if I wanted to allow me to look closely at him, but if I had ventured to tear a few leaves someone would surely have shot me.

We had come down from the plateau, nature had other colors and it was hot. Nabil pointed me to an abandoned farmhouse. The Chinese engineers and workers had lived there that they had built many roads, including the one we were on. He showed me land that someone must have once farmed. Now it was barren. The Chinese had introduced new models of agriculture, but then they started brewing their own beer, great beer, and sold it to the people. The government had kicked them out and the farm was dead.

The Sheikh woke up in Taizz. I observed that he had missed a nice trip: he replied that nature interested him little because it was always made up of trees, flowers and stones.

We stayed in an old and dirty hotel.

The Sheikh asked me to accompany him to the chief merchant of the qut. The man lived in a new building. We found it in the mafray. Near him many others chewed qat. An old man sitting on a stool crushed some leaves in a small mortar, reduced them to a pulp and then put them in his mouth with a spoon.

The old man raised his head, smiled at me. He had no teeth. The chief motioned for us to sit down and offered us the qat. We chewed in silence, I without any pleasure. The chief murmured something to the Sheikh and he whispered to me that we had to leave, we had an appointment. There was a mosque nearby. We entered. It was very old and had beautiful carpets. The imam came to meet us. I noticed that his left hand was missing. The Sheikh asked me to wait outside with Nabil. After a few minutes he went out. He looked satisfied.

«I concluded an excellent deal and in a short time. I got what I wanted and I didn't pay a dime.'
"How did he do?"
He didn't answer me. I had an intuition: "Did he kill the imam?"
"When you think of death, everything becomes ridiculous."

We returned to San'a without speaking. On the plane, the Sheikh recited: «Today your head is swollen with many illusions, deceived by fools. When then, in a tomorrow, abandoned, you need help, come to this friend».
I asked him: "Are you this friend?"
«Father Matteo, the false friend is like the shadow that follows us as long as the sun lasts.»
"He did not answer me."
"Are you sure of that, my friend?"
"What did we go to San'a for?"
"Didn't you like the trip, Father Matteo?"
"Yes, it was interesting, but what was the reason?"

"Recover this item."

He pulled a tiny cassette from his pocket and slipped it into a portable player.

He said: "Now take a good look, please."

I saw a car driven by an Israeli officer. I knew that street well, it wasn't far from the American Colony. The officer, who looked familiar, got out of the car, shook hands with three young Palestinians, then set fire to the car with them. At that moment Father Silvestro arrived, who checked that the car was burning properly and then walked away, calmly, with the three boys and the Israeli officer.

I had once seen a paleontologist friend reconstruct the complete skeleton of a prehistoric animal from fragments of fossilized bone. He had worked for almost two years and I was amazed at the enthusiasm that had never failed him throughout that period. As the Sheikh looked at me, I finally understood the nature of my friend's enthusiasm. It was the same as he now felt towards me. He had unearthed a fragment of a complex story that astounded me.

«Father Matteo, did you understand who the officer is?»

I didn't answer.

«Come on, Father Matteo, a little effort.»

"It's the Good Soldier," I exclaimed through clenched teeth.

"Good, it's Shlomo. And as you know, Father Matteo, Shlomo is a sort of adopted son of his Keeper."

Reverend Father, here is the report of the trip to San'a and the astonishing conclusion. I don't think I need to add anything else.

Please accept my most respectful regards.

Ayden melton.

CHAPTER ELEVEN THE GOOD SOLDIER AND HANAN

The Custos welcomed me into his private chapel early in the morning. He had just celebrated mass. I followed him into his study. He was limping and I noticed great fatigue in his movements. I offered him my arm, he shook his head.

«I can still walk by myself, the good Lord allows me. You know, I'm like those Christians of Nazareth who insisted on repeating to those who didn't believe it that the house of the Madonna was there where we had built our basilica. The scientists argued that the proofs were lacking and they replied that faith is stronger than any proof. When the scientists finally dug up, they found not a cemetery, as they thought, but houses. One had become a place of worship and on the walls of that Christian synagogue I read a prayer, "Hei Maria", written by a pilgrim who had prayed in that holy place.

Father Matteo, I am like the pilgrims to whom faith had suggested that Mary lived there, and not like the scientists who demanded proof. And so it is with my legs. Doctors say it's clinically impossible for my legs to move, I answer that they go ahead with blows of faith and not science."

In the study, he leaned back in his chair with relief. His legs were swollen. She asked me if I wanted anything to drink. He wanted a fresh orange soda. He pointed to a carafe on the desk. He suggested I drink it too, without sugar like him.

"It's better for digestion. Did you hear about the landslide in front of Herod's Gate, near the Islamic cemetery? All that land on that bar, how many dead! I went to bless them, Christians and Muslims. Do you know what amazed and moved me? Solidarity. Jewish soldiers were digging to save buried Palestinians from the landslide. I certainly don't want to say that peace can be built with natural disasters, but undoubtedly opportunities for solidarity bring knowledge and cohesion.

Many, Father Matteo, are fighting this war without knowing how it started. Try asking a Palestinian or a Jew why they hate each other. They will answer that they hate each other because they have always hated each other, it will be difficult to find someone who remembers the origins of hatred and, even when they find it, they won't offer plausible explanations. Hate exists in memory as a habit, you understand? Is it possible to eliminate habits? I believe so, with reason, with love and above all with solidarity. That's why those dead for once were useful. The urgency of material things has made hatred forgotten.

I reminded him that in other cases it was exactly the opposite. Recently a group of Orthodox and one of Sephardim had argued at the Wailing Wall and had thrown banana peels and buckets of water at each other. And this showed how there was a great difficulty in relationships even within the same religion. He asked me if I had ever been to Nezarim. I told him no.

«Nezarim is a tiny territory of three square kilometers on the shores of the Mediterranean, right in the middle of the Gaza Strip. If it weren't there, but just five kilometers to the east, or fifteen to the north, it would be a beautiful place, ideal for a holiday village. Instead it is hell within hell. Nezarim is one of the one hundred and forty settlements of the Cousins of the Wall in Palestinian territory, and it survives only because it is guarded day and night by armored vehicles of the Israeli army. Until 1984 Nezarim was a military base. Then, after Sinai was returned to Egypt, settlers evicted from the kibbutzim arrived. Today there are almost two hundred. They are teachers, farmers, they have a gravel pit. They grow mangoes, grapes, sweet potatoes and tomatoes. But they live besieged by the Friends of the Rock. Teachers and other commuters working in Israel cross six kilometers of road into Palestinian territory every day. And at every meter there could be an ambush.

The path of dialogue, of faith, of solidarity is decisive for breaking down the sense of war. The Palestinians are Muslims, Catholics, Melkites. They have good relationships with each other and different reactions to injustice. In the face of hunger and danger, the Muslim becomes fundamentalist, the Christian emigrates.

In 1943, of the 200,000 inhabitants of Jerusalem, 30,000 were Christians. Today five hundred thousand people live in Jerusalem and there are ten thousand Christians. Father Matteo, I would like the strength of religion to be in truth and not in extremism.

I follow the Gospel, and I want and ask for justice for the poor. There are Christians in the Palestinian Authority in prominent positions. There are Christians in prisons and every parish has had at least one death."

The Keeper took a deep breath and looked at me for a long time. I was so used to his monologues and his pauses that I waited in silence for his next words. He asked me paternally: «How was his stay in that sea of Galilee, where Peter and Andrew were called by Our Lord to catch men and no more fish?».

I spread my arms. Maybe she hadn't read my report, I thought. He continued: «In his Gospel, Mark recounts Jesus' journey on the Sea of Galilee. The storm breaks out, Jesus saves the boat and its occupants by ordering the wind and the water to calm down. During his journey, Father Matteo, the wind blew a lot and the waves were high. I don't want to say that you behaved like Jesus, but you did a small miracle».

He paused, I took the opportunity to thank him. He continued, "Yemen is a harsh and fascinating country, isn't it?"

«Please, Reverend Father, let's go in order. I have to connect, with his help, many apparently unrelated facts. »

"Shall we start from the last one?"

"All right."

'Your journey with the Sheikh was a little careless. Do you understand who you work for?"

"No, but I know part of his life in Argentina."

"I guess he didn't tell you everything. Did you explain to her what she does for a living?"

"No."

"It will be a surprise when he finds out."

"The surprise was that filmed document."

"It's irrelevant."

"Is it irrelevant that the Good Soldier agreed with Father Sylvester?" He didn't answer.

"Reverend Father, I have a feeling you knew, and told me of something else."

"I didn't know the details."

«The real reason for Father Silvestro's exile is not his small and harmless personal Intifada, but that strange story. You didn't tell me the truth, Reverend Father. I almost feel like quitting Discreet."

"Almost?"

The Keeper's question left me dumbfounded. Why did I say almost? I realized that I had given him quite an advantage over me. I thought I caught a glint of amusement in his eyes and I asked him what was the reason. Patiently, but also decisively, the Keeper said to me: "There is something you stubbornly don't want to understand."

"What, Reverend Father?"

"You have a mission to accomplish. You are a priest and you must be true to your imagination of yourself, and if you are true to what you imagine, this is your truth about yourself. I think it always starts with dreams. But remember: without memory there is no life. Our memory is our coherence, our reason, our feelings, our actions. Without it we are nothing, Father Matteo."

The Keeper smiled for a long time. I told him his words were fascinating, but they didn't explain the latest events.

"What do you know about the Ark of the Covenant?" he asked me. I replied scholastically.

"It was a chest of acacia wood four feet long and two feet wide, lined inside and out with gold foil. The Ark was closed by a gold plate, on the plate two cherubs. Inside were kept the tables of the Law, a pot of manna and Aaron's staff. It was built a few months before the Jews left Egypt. Solomon kept it in the innermost part of the Temple, and when Nebuchadnezzar destroyed Jerusalem in 586, the Ark disappeared. Some historians believe that it had already disappeared before that date along with the Temple treasure.

«Very well, Father Matteo. This is what is known and must be known. But I make you a revelation. Instead, it is possible that the Ark is buried in the caves of Qumran."

"Where were the Dead Sea Scrolls found?"

"Indeed."

"And do the Cousins of the Wall know that?"

"They know there is a map."

I was more and more amazed.

"Father Matteo, in your opinion finding the Ark today would matter?"

"It would revolutionize archeology around here."

"Are you sure of that?"

"I think yes."

The Keeper was playing with my doubts.

"The discovery of the Ark certainly wouldn't change the fate of the world. But it would represent an extraordinary source of experience and verification for us, for the Israelis and the Palestinians themselves.

'The history of the map,' continued the Keeper, 'is recent. It was found in Wadi Murabbat, eighteen kilometers from Qurnran. Someone had hidden it in that area during the second Jewish revolt. The man who found her died suddenly. The son, convinced that his father had committed a sacrilege and had died for his, gave her to his confessor, one of our friars, Father Giacomo, who in turn gave her to Father Luca. The latter immediately understood the extraordinary importance of the document. He told me about it when he was sure of its authenticity. And we decided to disclose the discovery only when it was appropriate."

"And now is it timely?"

«Father Matteo, there are many dangers even for us who live within an established faith, a faith that is our tradition.»

I wanted to be absolutely clear.

"Reverend Father, did you have the map in your hands?" The Keeper smiled good-naturedly at me.

"It's not very important. The one who should have read and deciphered it would have been you, Father Matteo.»

Finally understood.

«So she had studied and decided everything at the table. I had to work on the map together with Luca. And being Discreet for Cultural Affairs would have given me authority over Israelis and Palestinians."

«Father Luca had explained to me that he needed her to understand the map. There was something that didn't convince him and only the one he considered his best student, that is she, could find the key to the colored riddle, so he told me. »

"What is the colored puzzle?"

"I can imagine the drawing of the exact place where the Ark is buried."

"Where is the map, Reverend Father?"

"In Carlino's collar."

I was amazed. Such an important document in a dog's collar. The Keeper almost justified himself.

"Luca thought it was the best hiding place." Then she added: «But Carlino, as you wrote in your report, had no collar».

"Someone must have taken it, Reverend Father."

"Impossible," he said dryly. Then she looked down at her papers.

"What really happened in Capernaum?" I asked him.

"I believe you helped Mrs. Annie Deroche escape."

"Would you prefer that I leave it in Bialik's hands?"

The Keeper gave a half smile. Then he looked at his watch.

«Bialik is waiting for you, he has to talk to you. Her car is in the yard right now. Go."

The tone was peremptory. The driver was now almost a friend. He accompanied me to the Talmudic Institute. Bialik was in his office. In the air a strong perfume with a hint of cinnamon. He motioned me to sit down, his eyes were red, his beard was unkempt and he looked like he hadn't slept.

He sighed for a long time.

"Do you like this perfume?"

"Yes it is good."

"What do you know about me?"

«Nothing, Bialik. We never spoke, she and I. I don't know anything about her and I don't think she knows much about me. What the secret services know about a person is always partial. You may know where I studied and who I frequent, what my habits are and who my friends are, but you certainly do not know my life.»

"It's safe?" There was passion in his voice now.

"Anyway, you don't know mine either, you don't know it at all."

"Did you summon me to tell me about your life, Bialik?"

"Maybe to let her smell the perfume."

"It's good, I told you."

"I haven't always done this job. I chose him to help my country."

"It's the same thing for me in a way."

"But you're a priest, you have to pray for everyone."

"I pray for peace, Bialik, but we weren't talking about me."

"Listen carefully to my story. One day in 1850, an old Prague rabbi, Meir Bialik, looked at his wife and daughters with whom he was having breakfast and said: "I want to leave for Jerusalem; which of you will accompany me?". The wife replied: "I don't. I'm too fat to go on such a journey." The younger son, Shlomo, said he would stay with his mother. The eldest, a young master named Moises, had no hesitation and followed him. On 10 November of that year, with a trunk and five hundred florins, Meir and Moises embarked on the magnificent steamer America in Trieste. The journey

was not easy: a fit of nostalgia after the departure, a long stop in Alexandria waiting for another ship, a storm in front of Jaffa, the luggage wet by the waves, the landing on the shoulders of two Turks, a long caravan journey with pilgrims and tourists from Jaffa to Jerusalem. Saul Bialik stood up and recited:
"A twig fell over a fence and fell asleep. So I sleep.
The fruit has fallen – and what should I do with my trunk. What with my branch?
The fruit has fallen, the flower already forgotten. The leaves survive.
One day the storm will rage, they will fall to the ground, death».

There was tenderness and passion in Bialik's voice. He said, "These are lines from Moises. My great-uncle Moises was a great sweet poet. I come from the other branch of the family: the one that remained in Europe. My grandfather Ruben and my father Abraham were gassed in Dachau together with my mother, my sister Rebecca, my brother Isaac, our Austrian cousins, in turn cousins of Stefan Zweig, who committed suicide in horror of Nazism. I got married in New York to Sara Ostermann, two years my junior. We had grown up together, and our provident parents had sent us to the United States before the massacre began. Our two families worked together in the theater. They ran a cabaret in Prague. When Sara and I arrived in New York we were hosted by family friends, theater people of course.

It was patriotic necessity that led me to Jerusalem. I decided to live here because I couldn't tolerate someone wanting to exterminate us again. I discussed it at length with my wife. Sara didn't think we'd be useful around here. She thought my place, even as a Jew, was in the United States. It was our place, she said. Father Matteo,

I'll make you a revelation: by moving to Jerusalem I gave up on a good career».

Bialik took a breath as if he was about to announce something terrible to me or as if he was ashamed.

"A career as a singer."

"You, an artist!"

"In a sense."

"Bialik, you fascinate me."

"Don't make fun of me."

"I'm serious."

«I made my debut with a small but significant role in Anything Goes. Cole Porter considered me a good character actor. When my head touched my left shoulder, the audience laughed. Sometimes I played black roles, my voice resembled, said Jerome Kern, that of a blues singer. I gladly accepted those roles because, as a Jew, I felt as persecuted as the blacks. Sarah was a protagonist. In Kiss Me Kate! She was extraordinary. And in Can-Can she danced very well, she was more graceful than Ginger Rogers, she had more sweetness in the movement. We gave birth to a daughter. I wanted our daughter to be born in Jerusalem. I considered it a duty and a hope. The idea that people from the most diverse nations could build a state capable of withstanding infinite adversity was part of our ethics, and our return ethic was a life necessity for me. But Sara did not understand this. She was a pacifist, and in those years being a pacifist in the United States was equivalent to being a communist.

Hanan was born in New York. President Johnson had escalated the war in Vietnam. By that time, Sara had become a prominent peace activist. One evening she wanted me with her in her dressing room. She shook my hand and said: "Acting, singing is difficult. Protagonists are born and the public understands it immediately if you pretend.

When I'm on stage, I get feverish. And when I walk back into the dressing room after the applause, it's like I've come down from heaven. Alone, in that silence, in front of the big mirror that reflects my costumes, my objects, I stare at my eyes and I'm scared".

She said again: "Please, don't be sorry, I'm too tired tonight, I won't go home with you. I have to stay here. Give a long, deep kiss to our little girl. I love her so much".

I waited for her all night awake. The next morning the theater custodian found her dead. Her heart, the doctors said: the intensity of her feelings, I knew. I left for Jerusalem with Hanan. I raised her with love thinking about Sara all the time. I didn't want to love other women after her and I gave my affection, my tenderness, my life to my daughter. Father Matteo, are you able to understand what it means to raise a daughter in this country? I pulled her up with all the love possible, trying to make her understand our dream and how it was necessary to fight to achieve it.

Everything runs terribly in Jerusalem, only peace doesn't run. The kibbutz was our pride and our fantasy fulfilled. It represented a model of life and society, it meant working together for an ideal. In Ein Ziwan, on the Golan, they killed the idea of the kibbutz: there will be monthly salaries and differentiated according to productivity, overtime paid and even the education of the children will be left to the initiatives of the various families. In short, everything changes. Kibbutzim will become capitalist institutions, you understand? It is the end of the collectivism that represented our moral strength. And without collectivism and moral strength it is impossible to face the peace negotiations well.

The other morning, Father Matteo, I was walking

around the Old City. I often go to the Old Town. As you can imagine, I speak Arabic perfectly. I stopped in front of a shop at the Eighth Station of your Via Dolorosa. The master showed me some papers: taxes for the shop, taxes for the sale of objects; five thousand tax dollars, he complained. His workshop was full of wooden Madonnas and crucifixes. He no longer sold anything. The Jews, he told me, were well aware that there were few tourists because of the attacks, but despite this, they taxed him in every way on purpose. At your Fourth Station I saw a plaque in Hebrew on an iron gate. In the old courtyard there was a Talmudic school. And even though this was one of the controversial places,

On the same morning, I saw your Latin patriarch, Bishop Sabbah, arrive at the Holy Sepulchre. He was preceded by two guards wearing the costume of Ottoman dignitaries, the symbol of the ancient Empire. In front of the door of the Holy Sepulcher there was a squad of our police, pistols and handcuffs in their belts. All this impressed me a lot. We were the armed ones, Father Matteo, and the others seemed to bring peace. It was this image that gave me a terrible feeling about us and our role. The strength of a nation, I reflected, is not measured by land, but by faith and

the bravery. A compromise had to be reached with the Palestinians. I didn't have clear ideas about Jerusalem, but the image of us armed in front of the Holy Sepulcher had disturbed me.»

He changed his tone. It got tougher.

«My daughter Hanan is a teacher of Art History: good, intelligent and tolerant. Inside her there is a strong search for some kind of general understanding, yes, I can define it that way. Father Matteo, I know that dialogue must be sought at all costs, but Hanan has gone a little beyond my expectations and my ideas.»

"That is?"

"Hanan loves a boy his age."

"Did you prefer an older man for your daughter?" She stared into her eyes for a long time, in silence.

"You're a friend of mine, aren't you?"

"Are you sure of that?"

"Help me."

"How?"

"Hanan loves the Good Soldier." My amazement was evident.

"You met Hanan."

"Where is it?"

"To Capernaum."

"It's Annie!" I exclaimed in amazement.

"Father Matteo, I was in Capernaum to convince you to change your mind." I told him that love was not an idea. She replied that too many strange things had happened in those few days. I invited him to explain them to me, if she could.

"You know about Carlino's collar. You can imagine how much we care. It is fundamental to any peace negotiation. For ultimate peace. If the Ark is buried in the caves of Qumran, it means that this has always been our land. It is the fruit of a covenant with Jahvè. I talked about it at length with the Keeper."

"But with the Ark, your hardliners will get stronger."

«Father Matteo, all of us Jews will become stronger. The Ark at Qumran gives us the right of possession over what you call "occupied territories". We, as the Ark will testify, have been there since Jehovah gave Moses the Tablets. The Ark at Qumram is divine testimony to our claim. But if the Palestinians find the map, they will destroy it to erase our right."

"What does your daughter and Shlomo have to do with

it?"

"They have a plan for peace."

"And that's not okay?"

"It's a peace against us."

"Shlomo pretended to be lynched."

"It was a way to go underground."

"The Sheikh has the filmed document testifying to the truth. You obviously know the Sheikh."

"Yup."

"Who does he work for?"

He didn't answer me. Instead, he said, "It's the footage that needs to be destroyed, not the map. That's a big deal for the Keeper. How would you explain the action of that friar to Rome?».

"That friar is in Cyprus."

"Ayden melton, find Hanan and try to figure out if she's really in love with Shlomo. If their relationship isn't deep, my life will go on like today, maybe I'll try to be closer to her. But if she finds out that they really love each other, then I guess I'll have to quit my job. For Hanan and for her mother's memory, I'm willing to give up anything, but I have to understand if it's right. I can't go against my country, just as I can't go against my daughter." Bialik was looking over my head now.

"Do you still smell it?"

"Yup."

«A friend, every anniversary of Sara's death, sends me a bottle. It was my wife's favorite perfume. I massage her forehead and chest with this perfume: it's the most painful, but also the most tender, way of remembering her. Please help me, and help Sylvie. That little girl is innocent. What does it have to do with the utopias of her parents? Why does she have to pay?"

CHAPTER TWELVE THE WALK

Walking in the Old Town for me had always meant reflecting and dreaming, thinking about my past, getting rich with news and imagining my future. A walker is always accompanied by something spiritual that puts him in a position to welcome every unexpected encounter with joy and benevolence.

When I strolled through those narrow streets, sometimes dirty, sometimes scented with incense and spices, every idea was capable of chasing me and I was ready to offer it the space of imagination and memory. Ideas often took hold of me so convincingly that my head seemed capable of knowing the world.

That morning I had heard on the radio a sad story in which the privilege of a walk had been paid for with one's life. In the desert of Judah, near their village, two young Israelis were exploring caves. And some equally young Palestinians had stoned and then stabbed them to death before abandoning them among the stones. One dead is equal to another in statistics, but a Palestinian baby in swaddling clothes killed by mistake by a grenade is not the same as two adults stoned and slit their throats. There is a significant difference in cruelty. And furthermore the unwritten rules of the Holy Land explain that the two alive boys would have had more value. They were allegedly returned to their families in exchange for at least ten captive Palestinians and a large amount of money. But that had been a token assassination. He responded to a need for revenge that can only be explained by a sense of lost honour.

The Israelis, monotheists long before Islam, had never lost their honor because they had been massacred in every century and had never bowed their heads until they had succeeded in creating a democratic society in the midst of monarchies and dictatorships.

The Palestinians behaved like Samson, desperate for the loss of their power. The killing of the two young men had the flavor of an act of impotence or even suicide.

So I came out of the Flagellation with the sole thought of letting my mind wander. In front of our entrance, on the other side of the Via Dolorosa, a Tsahal patrol made up of a non-commissioned officer and two soldiers was permanently on guard. They guarded the iron door of the tunnel that connected that stretch of the Via Dolorosa with the Wailing Wall and which ran under the houses in the Muslim quarter. From the door, closed at night and open during the day, groups of noisy and rude tourists came out, offending the sacredness of the place and above all annoying the concentration of those who, like me, had the windows of the studio on the courtyard of the Flagellation, near the Via Dolorosa .

The non-commissioned officer and the two soldiers had transformed the open-air guard post into a sort of small catering station for their own use.Contrary to usual I stopped to greet them. The non-commissioned officer, all taken up with cleaning the machine gun, didn't answer; the other two smiled at me. The younger one rhythmically waved an old newspaper to keep the embers burning under a small burner on which the coffee pot was boiling. He applied himself to his work with meticulousness and precision and his embers remained compact, without ash and incandescent coal flying around.

The third waved at me and asked me if I'd like a coffee. I answered him with a slightly provocative tone that I liked Italian coffee. He replied that he hated Nescafé and all those American substitutes, that he greatly preferred the Italian but didn't have the right machine and had to settle for the Turkish one.

His manner seemed to me that of an expert on the subject, who with firm kindness had put me right. Not to be outdone, I then told him that the coffee in my town, which was called Ginostra, was the best in the world. He asked me where it was, I explained it to him, he was very impressed that I was born on a small active volcano and the inhabitants lived in houses built on its slopes. I told him about prickly pears. He had never seen them. I told him about their full, strong flavor and how an inexperienced person could fill his hands with thorns. But it was worth it because the fruit was nutritious and also quenched thirst. And if you ate it ice cream, the sweetness refreshed the palate and the stomach. I described to him the capers that flavored the spaghetti, the women of Ginostra gathered them when they had time. There was one in particular, a widow with children in the United States, who went to capers every day. I explained to him that they were plants that loved the sun, there were many of them in Ginostra, and the flower buds pickled in salt or vinegar were a spicy and tasty condiment not only for pasta: they could also be eaten with bread, as if they were a dish. But they made me very thirsty.

"So afterwards," he said to me with the air of someone who had understood everything, "you eat frozen prickly pears and you'll be thirsty."

He wanted to know if Ginostra's sea was transparent.

«Our sea is so transparent that you can see the bottom even at ten meters away.»

He asked me how the bottom was. I replied that there were many dark stones precisely because Stromboli was a volcano. The soldier sighed for a long time. He lived in Tel Aviv and the sea wasn't very nice there. There were too many constructions near the beach. I

drank the coffee, I told him it was good. Satisfied, he offered me a stool, it was an Arab stool, the kind you carry with you, the seat folded under the
arm, the legs fixed to the seat with small wooden clips.

I found it a little funny to sit in front of the door of my convent, but I considered it an act of courtesy towards her. Probably the soldier thought he was kind to host me.

The non-commissioned officer mechanically continued to clean the machine gun, blowing with his mouth and spitting on the spots that seemed less shiny to him. He was now singing a song I'd never heard but knew a line from: "Next year in Jerusalem."

The coffee soldier explained to me that many songs began with those words, it was an aspiration, an ideal, a promise made to oneself, to Israel, to one's loved ones. The brothers sang that of the non-commissioned officer before entering the gas chambers. I had a snap. I wanted to ask him, "Is it possible that you can't get over the Holocaust?"

I held back. An endless discussion would ensue. The coffee soldier told me that he was born in Gush Katif, at the extreme south of the Gaza Strip, right on the border with Egypt. His parents were settlers, here they were all settlers spread over a dozen towns, two seaside resorts and a tourist village. There was a small airport and the economy was based on the greenhouse cultivation of flowers, fruit and other agricultural products which were exported to Cyprus, but also to some Arab cities. He proudly explained to me that Gush Katif salad was famous throughout Israel because it was guaranteed to be free from worms thanks to skilful genetic crossbreeding. I observed that salad is usually without worms. He didn't reply, he sighed and told me that Gush Katif flowers were shipped all over Europe, especially

Holland. And in a model farm, in the middle of the desert dunes, the settlers obtained from a hundred cows a large quantity of milk which was transported every morning to Tel Aviv in tankers. In the capital Nave Dekalim, he continued proudly, there were kindergartens, elementary and middle schools, high schools, two synagogues, one Sephardic and the other Ashkenazi, industrial workshops, palm trees and lawns. But for some time now the people of Gush Katif have been suffering attacks, revenge, stones and bullets. The perpetrators of that barbarism were the inhabitants of the Palestinian camps of Khan Yunis and Rafiah. And then the army, to make the roads to Gush Katif safe, had cut down the houses of the Palestinians and also all the trees. In the capital Nave Dekalim, he continued proudly, there were kindergartens, elementary and middle schools, high schools, two synagogues, one Sephardic and the other Ashkenazi, industrial workshops, palm trees and lawns. But for some time now the people of Gush Katif have been suffering attacks, revenge, stones and bullets. The perpetrators of that barbarism were the inhabitants of the Palestinian camps of Khan Yunis and Rafiah. And then the army, to make the roads to Gush Katif safe, had cut down the houses of the Palestinians and also all the trees. In the capital Nave Dekalim, he continued proudly, there were kindergartens, elementary and middle schools, high schools, two synagogues, one Sephardic and the other Ashkenazi, industrial workshops, palm trees and lawns. But for some time now the people of Gush Katif have been suffering attacks, revenge, stones and bullets. The perpetrators of that barbarism were the inhabitants of the Palestinian camps of Khan Yunis and Rafiah. And then the army, to make the roads to Gush Katif safe, had cut down the houses of the Palestinians and also all the trees. The perpetrators of that barbarism were the inhabitants of the Palestinian camps of Khan Yunis and Rafiah. And then the army, to make the roads to Gush Katif safe, had cut down the houses of the Palestinians and also all the trees. The perpetrators of that barbarism were the inhabitants of the Palestinian camps of Khan Yunis and Rafiah. And then the army, to make the roads to Gush Katif safe, had cut down the houses of the Palestinians and also all the trees.

"We Israelis, famous for planting trees, have now uprooted them. Don't you find it terrible?"

I nodded in understanding and he smiled satisfied. He offered me some coffee again, I thanked him by refusing it and set off along the Via Dolorosa without pretending to imagine Jesus.

I passed a number of stalls full of vegetables, flowers, fruit, rye, oats, wheat. I stopped in front of a lumber yard with logs and chips and then in front of veiled women engaged in modest trades. They sold garlic braids and dried chilies. I was enchanted by meeting a small apple tree grown in a crack in the ground.

As thoughts and ideas came and went like flashes of light, Sylvester came towards me. It was an unusual and formidable apparition that almost completely obscured my thoughts. I didn't expect to find it in that market. I only managed to ask him: "Why are you here?"

He looked at me and it seemed to me that I was a dwarf that he could easily have trampled on. I felt the same emotions that invaded me in Ginostra when, I was five or six years old, I met Tommaso, a gentle giant, stupid and harmless, who, however, scared me a lot. Actually I was small and he was probably normal height, but he looked to my childish eyes tragic, monstrous and immense. Tommaso communicated with gestures and blocked the path that led to the sea, preventing me from making any movement in my attempt to speak.

Now the apparition told me that for Silvestro there was no peace. He didn't sleep in a soft bed, he didn't live in a cozy and comfortable house. He lodged everywhere and nowhere. His current life was devoid of happiness, of love, of human joy. No one was interested in his events and his existence. Past, present and future were for him like an unpopulated desert. In his eyes shone the anguish of buried worlds and a distant pain appeared in his every gesture. He wasn't old and he wasn't young. It seemed to me that he had a hundred thousand years behind him and that there was no flowery grave for him anywhere.

"Goodbye, my friend Silvestro" I murmured to myself, "try to have a good time anyway."

Without looking at that ghost again, because I had clearly dreamed of it and Sylvester must certainly be in Cyprus, I continued on and soon reached a small square where a small crowd was being harangued by a young man with an inspired air. They were Palestinians. I heard shots and, before I knew what was happening, two military trucks appeared. The Friends of the Rock fled, pursued on foot by the soldiers.

In fearful silence, while many merchants had lowered the shutters of their shops, I made my way to the Wailing Wall. I was to meet a Jewish archaeologist and work out some ideas with him for a seminar in Paris which we were both to attend. The seminar had as its theme the authenticity of David's tomb in the area of the Last Supper. The grave was fake and my friend knew it. But he couldn't tell. We had to invent something to allow him to emerge with dialectical elegance from his personal and scientific embarrassment.

I arrived a few minutes early and waited for him sitting on the long, narrow stone bench that borders the area under the houses in the Jewish part of the Old City. Until 1967 there was a tangle of hovels that formed the North African neighborhood, razed to the ground to create the vast esplanade at whose extreme limit is the Wailing Wall.

Tourists who want to observe the Wall from a distance and also want to rest usually stop on the bench. I was looking at the small groups of Orthodox, with black braids, black clothes and children all strictly black, who hurried back to Mea Shearim after prayers, and I thought that also because of their variable moods, peace was difficult. A dozen young soldiers took their places next to me. I assumed they came from some war zone. One of them was blind. On his cheeks the soft, pale shadow of a beard that hadn't yet met the razor. His face was broad, his features flat, on his forehead the scar of the wound that had robbed him of his sight in some battle. His closed eyes gave his face an air of absence. He sang a song in a low, sweet voice accompanied by a small accordion. He sang more, and all the words spoke of his love for a girl whose mouth, nose, eyes he would never see again. Her voice communicated pain and sadness for the life that was fleeing with war and death.

I looked at the boy's companions. They listened to him motionless, silent, hostile towards the Friends of the Rock. I felt immense pity and thought that there was no way to compensate for the suffering of the young soldier. It was at that moment that I understood how that boy was not a Jew, but an inhabitant of the Holy Land and had the right like the others, the Palestinians, the Syrians, the Lebanese, the Jordanians, the Egyptians to live in peace.

"I was at the Wailing Wall praying, you know?" Bialik said appearing next to me. And he added, "You feel sorry for that boy, don't you?"

I said yes and told him in a burst of intimacy how a kind of sweetness, combined with a touch of bitterness, had invaded my heart at the thought of how many Israelis were suffering in Jerusalem. And I wondered how long they would be a prisoner of their own anxieties, tying so much of their money and creativity to Tsahal. Was it because strength had become a value in itself and they had forgotten that it was only meant to serve as a means of maintaining life? Or perhaps they no longer knew that living meant not only protecting borders but also taking care of the quality of the working day, the rights of the weakest, in short, democracy?

Bialik looked at me gravely, he observed that I was right: the risk was that his people would eventually become like armor without the knight.

"And not the other way around," I observed.

Bialik replied that the opposite would be fortunate and then said: "Do you know what my mother said? "Everyone wears the face they deserve." And if my face were to express fifty years of Israel's life in a single expression, I would choose that November 4, 1995 when Rabin on stage in front of the crowd sings the song of peace. I was not far from him at the time, and I assure you that his was the face of Israel. On his face appeared the cardinal points of our history, the Kaduri agricultural school, the Palmach, the convoys that opened the road to besieged Jerusalem, the six-day war, Entebbe, the signing of the peace accords with the Palestinians and with the Jordan. I sang the peace song with him that Saturday night and thought he brought us life.

Father Matteo, that moment enclosed our strength and our weakness, the vitality and the courage to overcome fears. But he also hid the fanaticism that lurked with the killer gun in hand.

People who come to our country to understand how things really are, after a week they return satisfied to Europe or the United States and think they know. Understanding is impossible, there is nothing to understand. The only truth is that we are madmen with a vocation for suicide."

I looked at him puzzled. He continued, "You don't believe me? For years the whole country has been a huge construction site. In a cloud of dust, between bulldozers, bulldozers and gigantic trucks, the landscape is transforming especially along the axis formed by the two new roads: the Allon Road, which from Jerusalem runs along the Jordan valley from north to south parallel to the river, and the Transamaria, which connects Tel Aviv with the heart of the occupied territories. Near those roads, as on the hills surrounding Jerusalem, bizarre villages grow. From afar they look like majestic fortresses placed to guard the valleys that open at their feet. Two of them protect Jerusalem, make it impenetrable, ours forever. I don't think she ever visited the houses inside those fortresses. They are blocks of apartments which generally have a circular or polygonal shape, inside a courtyard which is accessed through a narrow door; the windows, the terraces, the balconies are designed to repel an attack, to place a machine gun and sell dearly».

Bialik sighed and concluded: «And then, Father Matteo, haven't I proved to you that we are madmen with a vocation for suicide? We Jews no longer have a biography to tell, but rather a destiny that nevertheless flees too quickly".

I was now walking towards Zion. I wanted to pray in the Sala del Cenacolo, I had been missing from that holy place for a few weeks. Before arriving, I saw a high wall with an open door. I entered a large garden of earth that looked like a carpet. Here and there in the silent air, from some hedge in which he hid and had built his nest, a bird let his voice be heard. A feeling of love for the universe invaded me, and sincere gratitude. There were pecotinas, figs, cherry trees. A concert of distant voices reached my ears, they seemed to me like children.

Moved by the wind, the sounds of a dear and distant world came back to my memory, of a garden placed on a small hill of black earth from which I enjoyed the view of the open sea. My father's name was Tommaso. An emblematic name. Our house was almost rich. He had inherited it from his father, on the ground floor a large kitchen with fireplace, radio, wood-burning oven, an old table that my father claimed was oak and the gas refrigerator that he had given my mother for Christmas of 1960. After dinner, he had wanted me, my twin brother and the two sisters, all four of us standing, to clap our hands as in the theater to celebrate that revolution at home. He, who loved beautiful things, he would not have been able to buy the new double bed with the wrought iron headboard which in his plans should have been a gift to his mother for Christmas 1961. He would have died at the end of March in a small street of Lipari overwhelmed by an unconscious and disrespectful motorcyclist . A few days later the letter would arrive that would change my life by offering it joy and wisdom. I would have gone to Assisi among the Franciscans to become one of them and then here I would have met Father Luca who would have taught me to excavate mosaics.

The kitchen, where much of our domestic life took place, adjoined the sitting room on the right, the main attractions of which were two Frau armchairs and a three-seater sofa upholstered in floral-patterned cretonne. The coffee table was missing between the sofa and the two armchairs and my father always said that he would have bought it in Milan. In my imagination Milan became not only the city of tables, but also the only city where they were for sale.

Upstairs were the bedrooms. The room where my twin, who died of a brief and defiant tropical disease while volunteering in Rwanda two years ago, and I slept, included two cots, two small desks, and a wardrobe. The smallest, where the sisters lived, had a bunk bed and a dresser. The sister who slept in the bottom bed is a nun in a nearby convent Pavia. The one on the top bed lives with our mother. She is ugly but has other qualities. She cooks well, she is a skilled seamstress and irons to perfection. She has been engaged for years to the barber of Stromboli, I promised her that I will celebrate their wedding, but she never decides. I am convinced that hers is an act of generosity. She doesn't want to leave her mother alone.

Crossing the garden I had arrived in the courtyard of the elementary school which occupied the lower floor of the building in which the Last Supper was located. Our religions mixed here, Jewish children learned to read where Jesus' last supper took place.

Now, in front of me was lying a big fat dog, funny, harmless and playful. His attention was captured by a child who, huddled on the steps of a staircase and frightened by him, indulged in prolonged crying. A woman, clearly a teacher, tall, beautiful, came up and, pointing to the child who was still crying, she said in a harsh tone, "Hey, you, see Isaac? He's a bad boy, he doesn't listen to his teacher."

I did not understand what he wanted from me. She went on, "Explain it to him," she almost screamed now,

"Tell him what you do in Palestine to children like him."

I was completely confused and could not speak. Evidently she had taken me for a Palestinian.

"You take them out of the house," she explained to me and him, seeking my approval, "then put them in small rooms, without food or water." He continued to tell how dark that room was, the child fell silent, now he was staring at me scared. Without waiting for my answer, the teacher turned her back on me and the boy ran after her.

I looked again at the garden and thought that sometimes, in spring or autumn, when the climate loosens its grip for a moment, in the Holy Land it is time for mercy. Mimosas, cassia shrubs and mustard fields flourish. Carmel is evergreen, Galilee is a sensual passage between mountains and valleys under the serene and thoughtful eye of the sea. Sometimes, precisely in places full of memories, a Christian like me feels the need to leave the main road and find some unknown path. It will be that sparse and sparse landscape that will give him some joy. In the Holy Land there are no thick forests, large lakes, or rushing rivers. There is only the small Sea of Galilee, whose level is closely watched by all due to the danger of drought, there are some woods with trees planted by the National Fund with the aspiration of creating a green illusion of Europe in the heart of the Middle East. There is only one river, a thin stream of water, the Jordan, which no doubt amazes the pilgrims who have magnified it in their dreams. But there is always a chance to find a hidden place, without dangerous settlements, weapons and stones.

I went up to the Last Supper. I prayed for a long time, luckily alone. There were no tourists or other religious. Prayer in a way refreshed me.

I thought of the intrigue I'd gotten into, and I got the

feeling that no one was telling me the truth. Not even the Keeper. I resumed my walk with these not very reassuring thoughts. I headed towards the Armenian quarter along the road that skirted the perimeter walls of the Old City. It was narrow and even cars passed through it. I heard a child scream, another child had thrown a stone at him legs. The wounded boy cried out in pain and rage, while the other boy fled, looked at me with a satisfied smile. He was dark in complexion, he could have been either a Cousin of the Wall or a Friend of the Rock. The wounded child was "Armenian and took refuge in the courtyard of San Giacomo il Maggiore. It was the church I loved most in Jerusalem, I especially appreciated the three naves and the solemn atmosphere.

A choir of monks had sung a sweet and poignant melody. When he finished they hurried towards the exit. I shook some hands thanking them for the joy they had given me.

I went on, passing through that small stretch of road covered by vaults to the left of which is the police barracks built where Herod's palace once stood. I smiled noting to myself how it really was the ideal place for a barracks. I was in front of the Citadel now, and I entered the narrow streets that led to San Salvatore. I stopped to pray in the Melkite church. I was kneeling and felt a hand on my shoulder. It was Monsignor Lahan. He told me that he was very happy to see me in his church. He considered it an act of devotion and respect. I got up and told him that I had been walking in the Old Town. I did it when I had to think about something.

"And what was your conclusion?" she asked me smiling.

"I was thinking, Bishop Lahan, about that time I came to see you and you were talking to someone on the phone about Carlino's collar."

"What do you want to know?"

"Who was he talking to about it?"

"But with the Keeper," Monsignor Lahan replied, as if it were the most natural thing in the world.

CHAPTER THIRTEEN VIDIGAL, LIE AND GUILT

Bishop Lahan kindly dismissed me. I realized how the tone of his answer, I don't know how much wanted, had blocked all my questions. But now I had an advantage over the Keeper. I knew he had spoken to Bishop Lahan about the Pug collar and I could use this news in my next meeting with him. After an initial moment of almost euphoria, I wondered if anything had changed. And I answered no.

I had an appointment with Father Vidigal at the American Colony. I could have gotten there much easier going through the Damascus gate, but instead I had preferred that walk to clear my mind. But I hadn't released a damn thing. And even that shadow which, aided by the sun, had turned into Sylvester had created disturbances in me.

Vidigal and I sat down at a table in the inner garden of the American Colony. A sort of paved courtyard on the ground and on the walls of ancient and very colorful tiles. The wrought iron tables, crowded with noisy guests, crowned the beds of violets and daisies and a central fountain full of fish and birds, which quenched their thirst after pecking crumbs and leftover food from the plates.

Vidigal managed to reassure me as always and, even when I told him about Silvestro and the Good Soldier and the mystery surrounding Carlino's collar, he said that in the Holy Land there were many incomprehensible things, anything could happen and nothing could change.

«You see» continued Vidigal, «I don't like this Jerusalem in which we live. I prefer Mandatory interwar

Jerusalem."
"What's left of her?"

«Almost nothing, and there are now few moments in which you can still smell it: at sunset, when the city turns pink, or late at night, when the lights of the Old City look like stars.» I asked him if he thought the future of Jerusalem was entirely Israeli.

"No, I see the Jerusalem of the future exactly as it is now, a torn city. There can be nothing in common except an agreement not to fight each other, a vulnerable truce, based on a low level of expectations. Matthew, a political partition of Jerusalem is not possible. These are ideas that come from those who want a clear-cut, precise solution. The truth is, Jerusalem has been destroyed forty times in the past. There must have been a reason, don't you think? Do you know why it is a city of the dissatisfied? Because it's a place for bigots and mad prophets. What compromise can you find around a place where Jews come from all over the world to pray, banging their heads on a wall that supports the esplanade on which Muslims recite the Koran? Do you have a plausible answer for me?"
I shook my head no.

«Matthew, Jerusalem is a symbol and symbols are by their nature indivisible.

They represent an identity, and a split identity leads to madness."

A waiter brought us tea. I hadn't ordered it but I drank it to please Vidigal, who kept shaking his head and muttering.

"Poor Jerusalem. Here everything is difficult and impossible. I've always wondered where I'd like to be buried. Where would you like your grave?"
I tried to joke.

"To the Holy Sepulchre."

"I see. I, on the other hand, in a place where the sounds of a primordial world arrive.»

"Did you find this place?"

"Not yet."

"Vidigal," I told him, "you must help me." He replied that, if he was within his means, he would gladly do it. However, he had to tell me a certain story that happened to a friend of his and on which he wanted my opinion.

This friend of his, Alfred tentatively called him, had been sent to Cairo on a certain assignment. There were winds of war in the Middle East. After taking over the hotel room in which he had been ordered to stay, he behaved like a tourist. The hotel had a vast and fragrant garden in which the restaurant was located. An attentive waiter informed him that after dinner, at no extra cost, he could watch a magical light and sound show. And that there was no need to fear bites from mosquitoes or other animals because at sunset his colleagues sprayed an effective, odorless insecticide. Alfred devotedly abandoned himself to the sensations. The beauty of the places exasperated him rather than thrilled him; and yet there was something cheerful about the landscape, a simple candor, which made him smile with pleasure.

Alfred traveled with a brand new passport, a borrowed name, and this gave him the pleasant sensation of possessing a new personality. He often felt a little tired of himself and was distracted for a time by the idea that he was simply a figment of the imagination of whoever had sent him to Cairo. After breathing deeply the air of the Nile, he ordered dinner in the garden and waited for the person he was to contact to appear. And finally Omar Ayoub, that was his name, appeared. He was a man of about forty-five, short, dark, graying hair, of medium height, massive, with a broad, anonymous face. He was wearing a shirt with a wide open collar and a gray suit. He was with his wife, a resigned and sad-looking woman. Omar Ayoub sat down at a table opposite Alfred's and loudly explained to the waiter that they had had an interminable trip. They had been driving to Al Fayum Oasis and had seen mirages. The waiter said he was born in the Oasis. Omar Ayoub observed that it was a beautiful place and asked Alfred if he had ever been there. Alfred, happy to be involved and to be able to get to know Ayoub in this way, said no. Ayoub began to describe the Oasis in great detail and Alfred thought that he was a good and pleasant conversationalist. At the end of the meal they were friends and watched the magical sound and light show over branded whiskeys. After the last glass, they said goodbye and made an appointment for the next day. They had been driving to Al Fayum Oasis and had seen mirages. The waiter said he was born in the Oasis. Omar Ayoub observed that it was a beautiful place and asked Alfred if he had ever been there. Alfred, happy to be involved and to be able to get to know Ayoub in this way, said no. Ayoub began to describe the Oasis in great detail and Alfred thought that he was a good and pleasant conversationalist. At the end of the meal they were friends and watched the magical sound and light show over branded whiskeys. After the last glass, they said goodbye and made an appointment for the next day. They had been driving to Al Fayum Oasis and had seen mirages. The waiter said he was born in the Oasis. Omar Ayoub observed that it was a beautiful place and asked Alfred if he had ever been there. Alfred, happy to be involved and to be able to get to know Ayoub in this way, said no. Ayoub began to describe the Oasis in great detail and Alfred thought that he was a good and pleasant conversationalist. At the end of the meal they were friends and watched the magical sound and light show over branded whiskeys. After the last glass, they said goodbye and made an appointment for the next day. happy to be called into question and to be able to get to know Ayoub in this way, he said no. Ayoub began to describe the Oasis in great detail and Alfred thought that he was a good and pleasant conversationalist. At the end of the meal they were friends and watched the magical sound and light show over branded whiskeys. After the last glass, they said goodbye and made an appointment for the next day. happy to be called into question and to be able to get to know Ayoub in this way, he said no. Ayoub began to describe the Oasis in great detail and Alfred thought that he was a good and pleasant conversationalist. At the end of the meal they were friends and watched the magical sound and light show over branded whiskeys. After the last glass, they said goodbye and made an appointment for the next day.

"At this point," Vidigal told me, "you will surely want to know who Alfred was and why he was in Cairo. Meanwhile, I'll explain who Omar Ayoub was. He was a Friend of the Rock born in Jerusalem but raised in Amman, where his family had taken refuge after the birth of the state of Israel. He officially he was a journalist. He had collaborated with an English newspaper in Cairo and with another in Paris. There he got into trouble for trying to get money through fraud and was sentenced to a light prison sentence. After his release, all traces of him had been lost for four years, so he had reappeared at a shipping agency in Marseilles. From there, still remaining in that branch of activity, he moved to Hamburg, where he got married, and then to

London, where he opened an office on his behalf, dealing with exports.

In London, he befriended a young Spaniard named Gomez, who was actually an Israeli agent. It wasn't difficult for Gomez to enlist him by offering him a monthly stipend. It was also easy to get him over religious and racial issues. Gomez was convincing. Ayoub, working for the Israelis, would not have betrayed his people, but would have favored peace. It must have been the good salary, or the need to get out of his difficult situation: Ayoub became an Israeli agent. After a trial period in Beirut, Gomez convinced Ayoub and his wife to move to Cairo. Ayoub was at peace with his conscience because he was actually passing false information to the Israelis. But they had noticed. Alfred was to warn Ayoub that the Cousins of the Wall knew he was deceiving them."

I asked Vidigal who had sent Alfred to Ayoub. He told me he would explain later and continued: 'Alfred needed a chance to win Ayoub's trust and sympathy. And the opportunity came. He had heard Ayoub's wife talking about the dervish dances and saying that she would have loved to see them. Alfred bought three tickets to the dervish theater show and invited the Ayoubs. They accepted happily and gratefully and admired the show. Finally Alfred asked Mrs. Ayoub: "Don't you think they transmit to the earth the divine energy that descends from the sky?".

"It is true!" Mrs. Ayoub exclaimed with conviction.

That evening, when they returned to the hotel, Mrs. Ayoub told her husband that their new friend, in addition to having been very generous in inviting them to the theatre, was endowed with a great artistic sensibility. Obviously Mrs. Ayoub knew her husband's business and was concerned about any new friendships.

But Alfred seemed to her more than reliable and passed on her conviction to her husband.

In those days an extraordinary performance of Aida was being prepared in front of the Sphinx. Ayoub, on the advice of his wife, to reciprocate the evening at the dervishes, invited Alfred. Alfred decided that after the show he would talk to him.'

Vidigal paused, then continued: 'Alfred was unable to tell him anything that evening. Because Ayoub wanted to invite him to dinner in a fish restaurant, not far from the Sphinx, and he spoke only of Verdi's opera, of the various editions he had listened to and especially of Obràida. He winked at his wife, who smiled conspiratorially. Obràida was Aida according to the people of Luxor, Ayoub explained, so they had mangled the title. And the two of them had been privileged to witness the performance at the Karnak temple. Unforgettable. She recounted the emotion of seeing the Triumph along the road of the sphinxes, with horses and camels. The extras were soldiers of the army stationed in Luxor, which is why they were so numerous and martial.

Alfred decided that he would speak to him the following day and alone. The next morning Ayoub died. He was out early, maybe he had to meet someone. His body was found not far from the hotel. He had a bullet in the middle of his forehead. Police said the shooter was a professional. Alfred asked Mrs. Ayoub if she had any suspicions. She claimed they had no enemies. And then she cried a long time in Alfred's arms. What would he do now?"

At the end of the story Vidigal was definitely moved. He told me that Alfred had experienced terrible feelings of guilt. And he explained to me that Ayoub, in the four years in which he had disappeared, had lived in

Jerusalem, in San Salvatore, making himself useful in a thousand ways: typist, archivist, printer, proofreader, electrician, plumber.

"He had become one of us, in a sense. Then one day he left Jerusalem and got married. But he always remained attached to the Custody and when he had the opportunity to earn a living making fun of the Cousins of the Wall, we didn't find it so unseemly. Then we learned that the Cousins of the Wall had discovered everything and had no good intentions towards him. For this Alfred came to him. Alfred long despaired of the failure of the mission. But the fault, in a certain sense, lay with the Custos at the time, who had chosen a friar that Ayoub did not know, and moreover was inexperienced. Poor Ayoub, he died innocent, really the news he passed on to the Cousins of the Wall was completely harmless.

"He was scamming them," I said.

«For a good purpose» Vidigal replied confidently and continued: «We must be very careful in our every action. It's terrible to do something you have to regret.'

I asked him if that story had changed his life. He looked at me amazed:

"Wasn't that you, Alfred?"

Vidigal smiled for a long time.

"Alfred was Sylvester's code name."

CHAPTER FOURTEEN OTHER REFLECTIONS AND SOME TRUTHS

Father Vidigal looked at me with some amusement as I shook my head. Then I said a sentence that made him frown: "It really is the city of mysteries."

"No, it's the Jerusalem of reality," he replied. And he added that the reality of the Holy City is that it always moves in the direction marked by the heartbeat. And his heart has three colors: the Christian, the Jew, the Muslim, and his reason has three faces: the Christian, the Jewish and the Muslim. Too often heart and reason do not coincide, and therefore the history of Jerusalem is richer in misfortune than in fortune. I observed that perhaps he was right. He added that Silvestro's human story must finally be clear to me. He had failed to save the life of a friend in danger and his guilt had accompanied him over the years. This was the reason for his commitment to the Good Soldier and the young Friends of the Rock.

I said that I had some doubts that at the basis of Silvestro's attitude there was only a sense of guilt and I was sorry that he hadn't confided in me. If he had told me the truth maybe I could have helped him.

Vidigal smiled affectionately and hugged me without replying. We said goodbye. I walked out of the American Colony feeling suddenly free and at liberty. A kind of late adolescence opened up in my soul with all its languor, tenderness and tears. I went to the Damascus gate. I was looking for wide places. I wanted to drink an immensity of air in a single breath, look at the sky, listen to the whispers of Muslim women, hear the choirs of young Orthodox priests, guess the age of the muezzin, do something poetic, dream of a future for those people

. I kept repeating to myself: free, they must be free, everyone is free here in Jerusalem. I wanted to do a thousand acts at once to help them win their freedom.

The smells of the Old Town shops warmed my heart. As I passed a cafe a wave of music came to me. I entered with my head held high. Many of the clients knew me. I greeted everyone with a gesture of the head that in my intentions should have been proud but friendly.

There was Muhammad sitting at a small table. He was inhaling smoke from a hookah with obvious pleasure. He told me that he was very sad because a close friend of his had been shot. It was Omar Kitheq, one of Arafat's personal guard commanders. He had been arrested in front of a school in Gaza while he was grooming a child and had been executed immediately, without trial.

As he spoke to me, explaining that it had certainly been a terrible misunderstanding, I remembered that Omar Kitheq had recently come to see me at the Flagellation to tell me of his post in Arafat's personal guard and that I could consider him at my disposal if I needed anything .

I had met him years earlier while traveling on an old and smelly bus that connected Jerusalem with Eilat. In the square from which the coaches departed, a great crowd was agitating. Whole families were camped out on piles of baggage, men running here and there and gathering in small groups to talk to each other. Some women screamed, others wept silently as they watched their husbands engaged in animated discussions. The general scene was one of indescribable confusion. It was early in the morning, the light was weak and cold, the faces of the people looked like the white faces of the dead, awaiting the final judgement. I found my bus. He was already full; a man said to me: «He Sit next to me, please. A whole family wanted to settle next door, husband, wife and a baby still in swaddling clothes. I already imagined a terrible journey. And then I know her."

I replied that I was certainly less cumbersome than that family. He laughed and remarked that he would be really happy to have me as a traveling companion. His name was Omar Kitheq, he was headed to Eilat. I packed my luggage and shook his hand. Omar Kitheq was a very thin man, with a bony face, large pale green eyes. When he took off his keffiyyah to wipe his sweaty forehead, he revealed a bald, bumpy skull.

We finally left. He told me that he had great respect for me, he knew me by sight, he knew I was a friar and an archaeologist. He used praise as if it were a natural and authentic function of being human, as others breathe and digest food. Not because he had something to say, but because he couldn't help it. He spoke in a high-pitched, nasal voice and with even intonation, constructing sentences with precision and vocabulary. He never used a short word when a long one was more appropriate.

I had never known so much about a person and not only about him, his opinions, habits and conditions, but about his wife, his wife's family, his children, their schoolmates, relationships with the best families of Jerusalem. He considered the Jews to be intruders who had occupied Palestine for the last hundred years.

Omar Kitheq was very fond of his wife and went on to exasperation to tell me what an educated woman and perfect mother she was. Unfortunately, he was in poor health and had undergone various operations, which he wanted to describe to me in detail. He had two sons who were still in school and was seriously considering whether to operate on them too. One had oversized tonsils, the other had appendix problems. A friend of his, the most renowned surgeon in Gaza, had offered to operate on them for free. Omar Kitheq showed me some photos of his wife and boys. He changed the subject and told me he hated cards.

"I wonder how an intelligent man can waste his time playing cards."

He further told me that he was a diligent reader. He underlined with the pencil the periods that piqued his interest and commented in the margin on what he had read.

When we arrived in Eilat, he assured me that we would meet again. And in fact he had come to see me. How could that same person lure children? I, that me I thought he had a fair knowledge of the human soul, I considered it impossible. I exclaimed, "Muhammad, they are wrong."

Then I asked him why he knew him well. Muhammad smiled.

"I'm going to tell you something that should have been kept secret. But he's dead now. Years ago we were sent together to Cairo. I remember there was a representation of your Ai from in front of the Sphinx. We certainly weren't supposed to see Aida but deal with a certain character who had done something wrong.»

I was white in the face. He asked me, "What's wrong with you?"

"Nothing," I replied. "Go ahead."

"There's not much to tell," Muhammad continued as he inhaled his hookah.

"Omar did that thing. I helped him, we went home."

I asked him what that thing was. Suleiman, holding the hookah as if it were a stick, waved it in the air.

"But what do you care?"

"Curiosity."

"Priests shouldn't be curious."

"I am a curious priest."

"We planted a spy."

"What was his name?"

"If I had to remember all the names of the ones we fixed!" Muhammad exclaimed. "Anyway, I can tell you that it was Omar who did it. I had accompanied him as backup. The spy was passing false information to the Israelis. But he was causing us problems because he fidgeted too much. He talked to everyone, it was annoying. I didn't even see his face. He was a flea and his fleas are crushed. »

Suleiman began to laugh.

«Just think that Omar told me that the flea, before being crushed, exclaimed: "Obràida, Obràida".»

I no longer wanted to talk to Suleiman. The deaths chased me. Or was it me chasing them. I went to the Holy Sepulcher because I had promised some pilgrims to bless their rosaries on the Stone of Anointing. I considered the act of blessing more serious. But I was convinced that faith also needed small detours and modest sacrileges.

I got back on the road. I felt deeply unhappy, I looked up, I saw all the windows closed, a sense of bewilderment began to spread over me again with a particular flavor that I could not understand. I felt like I was convalescing, my body seemed lighter. I heard the bells ringing. They were those of our little church. They sang Vespers. I arrived at the Flagellation, I went up to the Study of Coins, the light was on. This baffled me. The doubt that I had made the wrong room flashed through me, but an instant later I changed my mind. And I relived the scene from a few days before.

Scattered on the floor were some of my books, their

bindings in pieces. A slight noise to the right made me whirl around. I felt my heart leap into my throat.
Saul Bialik had a gun in his hand and a sweet, sad smile on his lips.

In a book I had recently read, the protagonist was faced with a gun-toting assassin. I asked myself: how would I react in such circumstances? And I had concluded that I was going to get so scared that I would lose my mind. Now, on the contrary, I didn't feel Afraid, perhaps it depended on the circumstances which were different. Bialik's attitude, who held his pistol as if it were a dead fish, was not threatening. Also, as far as I knew, Bialik wasn't a professional killer, even though he did a job where murder was allowed. Which, however illogical it was, had something reassuring about it.

But I, though not terrified, was still amazed and said, "Looks like something happened here."
Bialik gripped the gun more firmly.

"Do you mind closing the door?" he prayed kindly. "Just extend your right arm and you can do it without moving an inch."

The gun was aimed at me in a way that left no room for doubt. I obeyed, worried about getting hurt. I could already feel the doctor's hand trying to locate the bullet. I was afraid Bialik would let off an involuntary shot. I closed the door gently.

"What the hell does that mean?" I asked harshly. It was certainly not what I wanted to say, but I was almost shaking with anger. Bialik lowered the weapon and sat up.
"It seems to me that this is the second time, Mr. Bialik, that you have entered my office."
"You're wrong, Father Matteo, it's the first."
"Are you quite sure of that?"
"Sure," he replied. Then he continued. "It's very

embarrassing. I didn't expect her to come back so soon. I hoped I'd have time to tidy up a bit before I left.'
"Put your books in order, too, Bialik."

"Ah yes, the books!" he shook his head desolately. "An act of vandalism. A book is a precious object, a garden full of magnificent flowers, a magic carpet on which to fly towards unknown skies. I am sorry. After all, it was necessary."
"What was needed? What is he talking about?"

Bialik offered me a sad, resigned smile: «Please, Father Matteo, a little frankness. She knows it well. In this country, every inch of land and every stone must be watched."

"I don't think," I replied irritably, "that the situation in your country has any bearing on the situation in my office." Bialik sighed for a long time and exclaimed:
"Like a mother's love for her sick child, I will love you, my homeland!"

I shook my head. He continued: «Father Matteo, for me life in Jerusalem is always an adventure of the spirit: frustrating to the point of exhaustion, but indispensable. Jerusalem is the port of arrival for the nostalgia and hopes of eighty generations of Jews who lived before me. My daughter Hanan played, loved and argued in a language that hadn't been spoken for two thousand years, but for her and for us it came alive again. If our father Abraham sat down to supper in a house any, would understand the language we speak. Doesn't she seem like a miracle to you? There are more relaxing and less dangerous places in the world. Europe and the United States offer a more diverse life and culture. But in Jerusalem a Jew can realize his identity and confirm it day after day ».

I asked him, gently this time, what he was looking for in my study.

"There could only be one reason, and you know it as well as I do. I understand her embarrassment, of course.

He'll want to know my position. If it can console you, I find myself in the same difficulty: I wonder, that is, what is hers. »

I took a long breath.

"Listen well, Bialik. I go back to my convent, enter my study and find her waving a pistol under my nose. I have to conclude that he is a thief, or that he is drunk. However, thinking about it better, it seems to me that thieves usually don't meet their victims in the very place where they went to steal. As for the second hypothesis, you don't seem drunk at all. At this point, Bialik, I doubt you're crazy. If she is, I can't help but try to please her and hope heaven help me. If you, on the other hand, are still able to reason, I repeat that I demand an explanation. For the last time, what is this play about?"

He had listened to me narrowing his eyes.

"Perfect!" she exclaimed smiling. "Perfect! Father Matteo, for an instant I was almost convinced of his good faith. Almost. I would like to point out that it is not kind of him to try to deceive me, it is a waste of time."

I made a movement towards him. Maybe she misinterpreted it because he pointed the gun at me again. The smile disappeared from his mouth, his lips parted. I backed away.

«Father Matteo, I have the best of intentions towards you. But someone is forcing me into this interview."

"Who, Bialik?"

He stared at me almost surprised at my naivety. He explained to me that he had bosses, that it was always necessary to be vigilant, then he concluded: «I no longer find myself in a position to discuss on the basis of disinterested friendship, let's call it that. Let's at least try to be honest with each other.' He leaned forward slightly. Then, in an almost official tone, he asked me: «Why are you interested in Carlino's collar? Wait, don't answer me right away. I have no animosity, let me be clear. But I too have some interest in the collar. And now, tell me frankly what your goal is. Do you play in a team or are you a solo player?'

I did not find an immediate and plausible answer.

"Then?"

Bialik's smile was always sweet, but there was a cruel expression in his eyes and it brought to mind the image of a child ripping the tail off a freshly caught lizard.

"I can't promise you hell," I replied, "because it doesn't belong to your religion. But if you keep threatening me with that gun you won't get any response."

Bialik kept smiling.

« Well said, Father Matteo. The gun is useless."

"It was just to scare me, wasn't it?"

He admitted with a touch of shame that it was so. I then asked him if he had discovered Carlino's collar in the binding of my books.

"I was looking for an answer to my question. But all I've found is this." She showed me a sheet of paper. It was the plan of the mosaic of the church of Santo Stefano, in Umm-er-Rasas.

"I thought if you hid that plant between the pages of your books, you might have more inside your bindings." I explained to him that I usually put papers between the pages of books, but that didn't mean hiding them. Bialik observed that he could not blame me. I asked him if he knew what was in Carlino's collar. He nodded no.

"I'd be really curious to know if you know the Sheikh well, since he lives near the Nebo."

I didn't answer.

'I have a feeling I could tell you a lot more about the Sheikh than you could tell me. Now I'd better go » she concluded.

Calmly, I replied: "Good evening."

But instead of walking away he collapsed, putting his head in his hands. I didn't know what to do. "They've kidnapped Sylvie," she exclaimed.

I only now realized that his eyes were red and his beard was badly trimmed. I asked him if it was his nephew that he was looking for in my books. It seemed to me that I was being cruel.

«Father Matteo, what do you really know about me?»

"What you told me, Bialik. I can know where you studied and who you dated, what are your sexual habits and who are your friends, but your life is something much more complex. »

"What do you think of Hanan?"

"She struck me as an intelligent woman."

"I want to talk to Shlomo and Hanan, I have to understand them." I replied that in the meantime it was necessary to understand who had kidnapped his granddaughter. There was sun on the floor of my studio: a yellow streak, straight, very sharp. Bialik exclaimed: 'My sobs change nothing. But what can we change? Do our tears weigh heavily? Every man is an ordinary man to whom anything happens.

I asked him if he wanted to come to the refectory for dinner. She thanked me and told me that she preferred to be alone for a while. I greeted him telling him with a touch of irony that I wasn't accompanying him, he knew the way very well. Then I asked him, and if he didn't want to answer me I certainly wouldn't be offended, as he had entered the Flagellation. He showed me a kind of long key with few teeth. And he proudly told me that

Israeli technology was very high. With that tool, any door could be opened. I did not spare him my comment: «But not just any book. Now give me back the map of my mosaic.'

He did it with his head down, almost ashamed, and went away.

Monsignor Lahan was a guest at dinner in the refectory that evening. We talked about the dome of the Holy Sepulcher and the bad restoration. It was one of our favorite topics. Then he said to me, "Don't worry too much."

"About what?"

He looked puzzled.

«My good Matteo, you are intelligent but too emotional. Jerusalem needs coldness." Early the next morning, the Keeper sent for me. He had to speak to me urgently.

CHAPTER FIFTEEN THE KEEPER'S PROBLEMS

I had been waiting for the Keeper for an hour. I didn't understand why he had urgently called me and left me in the hall. It was the first time he made me wait. An elderly man came out of his study. I had never seen him before, in his right hand a bag, a kippah covered his head. He didn't surprise me to meet an Israeli in San Salvatore, he surprised me instead his expression. It was of sincere, deep pain. He was courteous, stopped in front of me, clicked his heels as if he were a soldier, and walked away into the corridor. I understood what he had puzzled me. The total physical and spiritual extraneousness of him to the place. The old Cousin of the Wall with the kippa on his head and the pained face somehow disturbed me. It was like a note fitting awkwardly into a harmonic musical situation.

Guillermo finally told me that I could enter. I scanned his face, he was impassive as always. I thought that Guillermo's first vocation had been that of secretary. And then as secretary he had heard the divine call and had become a priest. The Keeper sat at his desk as always. His face was pale and he had dark circles under his eyes as if he hadn't slept. He asked me: «Did he find the Good Soldier again?».

I told him no. Obviously, it seemed to me that she already knew this and the question had only served as an icebreaker. She gave a half smile.

"But I hope your research continues."

I replied that nothing was proceeding, on the contrary everything was getting more complicated every day and I had no news even of Carlino's collar.

"That was two years ago," the Keeper said gently. I

asked him what the matter was.

«I was with Father Vidigal, we had dined together. He was telling me about the project of a novel in the first person, in which the narrator, by omitting or distorting the events, would have run into various contradictions which would have allowed some readers to guess the reality. In the restaurant where we had dined, the one in the American Colony, where I think you usually meet with Father Vidigal, I realized for the first time that a mirror was in front of our table. I told this to Father Vidigal who observed that the mirrors contained something benign because they multiplied the number of people and revealed their miseries and pains. They were like sheets of immaculate linen, which covered up the shame and chased away the dead branches and moldy roots.

I observed that his poetic images were touching and convincing but not true. Indeed, perhaps it was just the opposite, the mirrors falsified reality and invented fictions. I reminded him of those amusement parks where one of the major attractions is the mirror maze. You enter, you get lost, you see your image multiplied too many times, you hit your head, you despair until you can get out of that hellish place. Vidigal replied that his novel would be like the maze of mirrors I had described to him. And in any case, without wanting to, I had agreed with him, because the labyrinth by multiplying the same image decomposed it and by decomposing it saved it.»

I asked the Keeper if he was trying to communicate something to me. She spread her arms and recited: «With bare feet and bare legs you are the agile grape harvester who is preparing to crush the red grapes in the steaming basin».

I replied that it was a bad image and I had no

intention of crushing anyone.

«Father Matteo, you have to fight falsehoods and intrigues. How would she feel if she saw on her altar the sacrament covered by an old and dirty veil? What would she feel if she could not kiss the divine house in any other way than through that veil?"

"I would suffer."

"Then?"

"I would try to solve the problem somehow. I don't know how yet."

"You're the one who has to draw your own conclusions. You have met all the protagonists of this story and perhaps you have understood that everyone is pretending. »

"You too, Reverend Father?"

"He talked a lot with Saul Bialik and I guess he formed an opinion of him."

I replied that my personal opinions were one thing and facts quite another.

"The facts, the facts, always the facts!" exclaimed the Keeper irritably.

I don't know what came over me. But I snapped and asked him forcefully: "Facts or fictions, Reverend Father?"

He didn't answer me, I then continued: «Reverend Father, I imagine that you continually look inside yourself and watch over your soul. She suffers and her suffering seems new to her. Did he ever notice? A man, an animal, a plant, anything presents us with its true appearance only once, at the moment of first perception. It's like she gives us her virginity. Soon after it is no longer that. Thus our senses transform, distort, obscure our soul. Do you understand where I'm going? What I tell you is the truth discovered by those who have spent years and years continually looking within themselves, only among men, only with the comfort of the Church. It is a much more important truth than facts. Facts, Reverend Father, are worth nothing.'

He sweetly replied that he didn't feel alone at all, he had never felt alone among men. And he asked me: «And you, has he ever felt alone in the midst of his stones and his mosaics?».

There was no genuine interest in the question. I limited myself to answering him that the mosaics were the work of men, but it didn't seem like a great answer. Then I asked him point-blank: "Do the fictions also concern Saul Bialik?"

"Maybe."

"Why was he in Capernaum?"

He wanted to know what Bialik had told me. I replied that he had told me about his life and his family. The Keeper looked at me strangely: 'And he didn't tell you about her older brother? Did he tell you that in Dachau he pulled the gold teeth out of the corpses before they entered the crematorium?'

"Was he a kapo?"

"He was one of those who beat, stole and were better off than other Jews because they agreed to collaborate with the Nazis."

I said that the brother's business was not relevant in Bialik's biography. He replied that it was part of his many pains and I had to take it into account. He continued: "Once Caliph Umar ibn al-Khattab besieged Jerusalem. Patriarch Sophronius went to the caliph and asked him for protection. The caliph then wrote a letter: "In the name of God, gracious and merciful. From Umar ibn al-Khattab to the inhabitants of Jerusalem. Security is granted on their persons, their goods and their churches so that these are not destroyed or reduced to places of habitation. I swear by Allah." The gate of the city was thrown open to him, and the caliph entered Jerusalem with his army. He arrived in the courtyard of the Holy Sepulcher and told Sofronio that he wanted to pray. And Sophronius replied that he could pray where he was. The caliph replied that this place was not suitable. Sophronius then had a mat spread out in the church. The caliph said it was no good there either. He made his way to the ladder that was in front of the church door and knelt down. Then he said to Sophronius: "I didn't pray inside your church because it would have been taken away from you and you would have lost possession of it. In fact, when I left, my people would have transformed it into a mosque because I had prayed there'».

I asked the Keeper why he had told me a story that "I knew well. He replied that by thinking about that historical event I could understand Bialik's behavior ". I reasoned aloud. Bialik had not entered the area of our convent in Capernaum so as not to create problems for us. If he had come in with the weight of his authority, he would have set a dangerous precedent. But I still didn't understand if Bialik had gone to Capernaum for the collar of Carlino. The Keeper replied that Bialik had gone there for his granddaughter. Then he shrugged.
"I've never actually seen that collar," he said.

I was amazed. But I couldn't reply. Because Guillermo entered without knocking and whispered something in his ear. The Keeper told me, "I forgot I had an appointment. Do you forgive me".

I left the Keeper's study perplexed by that haste. He had never interrupted a meeting like that before. Maybe he had to see someone and I didn't

I had to find out who it was. There was no one outside. I went down to the library to see Father Vidigal. Who didn't seem surprised to see me.

I asked him point blank.

"What's in Carlino's collar?" Vidigal answered me calmly.

«Helen, the mother of Constantine, found the Cross of Jesus in Jerusalem and took the three nails. One threw it into the sea, and it stilled a storm. The other two he destined for his son's helmet and horse bit. These precious relics have come down to us: now they are found in Carlino's collar and, even if a friar shouldn't say it, they have magical properties.

I felt a touch on my shoulder. It was Guillermo. The Keeper was waiting for me. I didn't ask how he knew I was at Vidigal's. I went back upstairs. I entered. He was smiling. He asked me: "Have you ever felt free?"

"Sometimes."

"Vidigal works his imagination sometimes, if you remember. Did he tell you about her new book?"

"No."

"He's writing his very own story of Helena, the mother of Constantine, and of Our Lord's Cross."

"Interesting," I said rather coldly.

"My legs hurt a lot. I spent a terrible night." I said I was very sorry and didn't want to tire him.

Sigh. Her voice was lower now.

"You knew that Omar Kitheq they shot, didn't you?"

I didn't ask him how he knew. He continued, "Poor man! Sometimes the Friends of the Rock are really cruel.'

"Reverend Father, to be honest, I don't think Omar Kitheq solicited children."

"But it's only natural, Father Matteo!" he exclaimed,

almost surprised.

"So?"

"Omar Kitheq was in Capernaum that night. And he tried to arrange with Bialik to hand over Hanan and the Good Soldier. He didn't succeed and they punished him."

I was puzzled. Omar Kitheq was no traitor. The Keeper looked at me with his usual smile. He wanted me to get there on my own.

"Of course." Now I understood: «Bialik set a trap for him, promising him something in return. But what? Carlino's collar, which he didn't have though. The end of the story was tragic. Omar Kitheq's companions were killed by the Cousins of the Wall patrol boat, I saved Hanan and Sylvie. Shlomo fled on his behalf, Bialik left empty-handed and retaliated by warning his counterparts on the other side that Omar Kitheq had betrayed them. To avoid a trial and excessive publicity, he was slanderously accused and executed.'

The Keeper told me that the reconstruction was right. But there was still something I didn't understand. Did the Palestinians know the contents of Pug's collar? And then there my impression was that Hanan was not very interested in the collar. The Keeper rolled his eyes.

«I believe that simplicity is the supreme aim of man. Can't you find it too, Father Matteo?»

I didn't answer. I left his studio with increasingly confused ideas.

CHAPTER SIXTEEN A FOLLOWING

I went along the Via Dolorosa with my eyes up to rummage in the windows of the houses where dinner was being prepared. It was sunset. Points of light winked around me. A light warm breeze had risen. I wondered why it had become an obsession why everyone was interested in Carlino's collar and everyone told me a different and unconvincing story.

I was near the basilica of Ecce Homo when I felt the sensation of being followed. I turned around and saw no one. The bells of a nearby church rang vespers, a muezzin intoned his prayer from a loudspeaker. A last ray of sun lit up my neck, a light wind brought me the passionate and recognizable notes of an ancient Jewish song. I was surprised that I didn't feel any tiredness. Around me everything went on with its own logic. There was a drop of water on my right cheek, but it wasn't raining. A tear, even though I had no intention of crying. But sudden memories had crowded into my mind which contrasted with the apparent placidity of the situation.

I remembered that time in the West Bank, when I arrived in a Palestinian village where the war had passed. The desert, the sun, the lack of water had contributed to the devastation. I had observed hungry men, mounds of mud where the houses used to be, heaps of sorghum where the streets once were, nests of snakes, dirt, carrion, dogs and mice that were no longer afraid of men. I was saddened by the sight of an immense and empty space where there had previously been a square. I tried to imagine it: lively, lively, with its spice, meat, vegetable and fruit market. Now instead it resembled the devastated circle of an ancient city, witness of a vanished civilization. Hard to tell who the ghosts were:

I realized that my emotionality was overtaxed. What was happening to me? I was in front of the Flagellation. I nodded to the soldiers at the guard post. The soldier in the café asked me if I wanted to have a drink with him. I thanked him. Then my attention was attracted by a procession arriving from the First Station. It was one of the usual processions in which pilgrims simulated Jesus' journey to martyrdom. Usually one of them carried a cross on his shoulders, obviously a light one. The soldiers didn't even look at them. Two brothers with habit and hood lowered walked to the sides. I absentmindedly noticed that not a single woman was there: the pilgrims were very young and almost certainly not European. I put the key in the lock, I opened the door and the two brothers slipped quickly into the courtyard before me. With some perplexity I closed the door, the two turned around and raised the hood. I was paralyzed with amazement.

"Father Matteo," Hanan said, "the procession is a mock. Those false pilgrims are Father Sylvester's boys, the same ones who burned Shlomo's car. Shlomo and I believe you can help us solve our problem."

"Because you're a friend of the Keeper," Shlomo said.

"Because she loves this country as much as we do and has good relationships with the people who matter," Hanan said.

"Because you work for peace and there aren't many people here who work for peace," Shlomo said.

"Because we know that revenge for her does not mean savage justice," said Hanan.

I interrupted them because I assumed that otherwise they would have gone on with more sentences like that and tried to bring them back to earth.

"Do you want something to drink, something to eat? I have bottled water, cognac, malt whiskey, biscuits, chocolate."

"I'd like some chocolate," Hanan said.

"Do you remember that passage from the Song of Songs?" Shlomo asked. And then he recited:

« My soul falls within me. Therefore I remember you, of the land of Jordan and of Hermon, of Mount Misar."

Hanan went on: «Winter is over, the rains are over, the flowers gush from the earth, the time has come for the gay refrains, in our countryside the turtledove coos, the fig tree bears its young fruit and the flowering vineyard gives off the its perfume".

"Our land is beautiful," Shlomo said, "and it must have been even more beautiful before the Turks killed the forests."

Shlomo and Hanan spoke with touching understanding and agreement. I hadn't noticed it in other couples. I wished Bialik would listen to them. He would have been moved too. They looked like two voices coming out of the same body, completing thoughts built together from time to time. Shlomo was the first time I had seen him well; in the film I had a fleeting impression of it and in Capernaum I had only been able to observe the back. He was tall, thin, with straight black hair. His blue eyes were the same shape as Hanan's. He interrupted them once again by telling Hanan that if he wanted chocolate we'd better continue talking in the study. They followed me in silence. In the Coin Study Hanan ate two bars of white chocolate and Shlomo drank mineral water. I warned them that I knew about Sylvie's abduction and would do anything to help them. Hanan smiled. Shlomo said:

«Our land is painted by an artist, think of the colors

that blend, the green orchards, the blond barley, the ocher yellow desert. Has he ever tried to lie down under an olive tree and let the sun warm his face? It is a normal thing everywhere, but here with us it has the flavor of history».

"Our land is small," said Hanan, "no more than twenty thousand miles. To go to Dan from Beersheba requires a week's walk, and two days from Nazareth to Jerusalem and one from Jerusalem to Jericho. Every hill, wadi, or village holds memories of the past. Canaan is sweet. The coast is straight and sandy and only the gulf of Haifa behind the promontory of Carmel allows ships to rest. And Jerusalem is sacred to everyone. Someone says that in Jerusalem, at night, even the jackals shout messages of faith and historical quotations. Jerusalem means city of peace, and instead it is the place where peace seems impossible.

"Father Matteo, you certainly followed the story of the street in front of the Jaffa gate," said Shlomo. «The clerics watched over the works, and in the Mea Shearim neighborhood they went around at night shouting "Gewalt" from a loudspeaker. Do you know what Gewalt means? It is a Yiddish word that warns us when something tragic is about to happen. A calamity. In this case the calamity was not the war, it was not the extermination, it was the fear that there were Jewish bones in the excavations of that road. And for the Haredim, digging up Jewish bones is Gewalt. The Haredim were willing to be killed for those bones.

"Gewalt," Hanan went on, "is the word that unifies all bones. The Muslim bones and the Christian ones and the Jewish ones. It's a terrible and right word. But there is another terrible and right word, Intifada.

"We," Shlomo said, "have Intifada. In Jerusalem, analogy wins. Everyone has his Intifada, everyone has his Gewalt. We do the same things using different words, and similar actions using words from the other vocabulary. We say the revolution in Arabic, Intifada, and the tragedy that is about to happen in Yiddish, Gewalt. The two words express historical moods and if everyone here had more imagination they could unite rather than divide.»

I interrupted them.

"Do Christians," I asked, "have a word that others might use?" Hanan stared at me wryly.

"Charity."

"But nobody uses it," Shlomo added.

"And yet," Hanan said, "we are of the same land and we must, we can be happy, because we are not different. We are from the same land and we have the same myrtles and the same brooms, the same mastic trees and the same acacia» they were now talking together.

Then Shlomo said, "But Jews and Palestinians live together avoiding each other as much as possible."

«Like two people» said Hanan «who are not husband and wife nor are they related by friendship and find themselves by necessity living in the same house, washing in the only bathroom, using the same kitchen and cannot leave. Father Matteo, do you want to know what it means to be a Jew, here, in the Land that you call Holy? Imagine a set table, there are plates, cutlery, glasses. No one would explain why the plates or glasses are on that table. Similarly we don't have to explain why we are here. But today, for the first time in our history, we are richer in fears than in ideals, and fears disturb our identity: therefore we need peace."

«Yes» said Shlomo, «precisely for this reason today we need to have the courage to commit ourselves to definitive gestures, in gestures that have symbolic value.»

"Like Ian Palach?"

They looked at me smiling and thoughtful.

"You might as well not die," Shlomo said.

"Because we love each other," said Hanan, "and definitive gestures don't mean death, on the contrary, far from it."

"And you will help us," said Shlomo, "otherwise we will continue to live in the nightmare of the pastry chef and in the memory of Rassan and Frieda's pain."

I asked who they were.

"The pastry chef from Ramallah," explained Hanan, "was ready to accept that one of his daughters be stoned because the law wanted it, and the law is wise. Rassan, a Palestinian Israeli who works at the University of Mount Scopus as a researcher, married Frieda, an Israeli Jew. Now they both experience that marriage as a sin.

"They," said Hanan, "must be sure that peace will happen."

Then Shlomo and Hanan did something that thrilled me. First they kissed passionately, then they held hands and walked around the Coin Studio as if they were in a park, looking at the walls, the windows, the objects. They approached, he hugged me, she kissed me on the right cheek.

«Father Matteo, we have fallen into a primitive tribal war, in which the only law is an eye for an eye, a tooth for a tooth: you killed one of mine, I will kill one of yours. In these parts, children are born between one funeral and another, in the midst of the blood of endless conflict. You can help us."

I felt them full of courage. Heroism, Hanan explained to me, is not a choice but a reflex. It's a function of the central nervous system, not a higher function of the brain. If she had thought about what to do, she would have ended up among the millions who have spent their lives in inertia.

"Jews and Christians are two branches of the same tree," he concluded. "If you always remember, it was the Romans who crucified Jesus."

"And the Holocaust," Shlomo added, "must remain in memory, but not fuel hatred." Hanan brought his face close to mine: "Father Matteo, we are undertaking a great undertaking."

"Help us," Shlomo added.

It was at that point that, to see their reaction, I said I couldn't help them in their search for Carlino's collar. They looked at me puzzled. Then Hanan exclaimed: "Father Matteo, I don't know if Carlino had a collar, but I certainly don't think it's a problem to find it."

Shlomo smiled at me sympathetically. I shook my head and almost stammered: "Sorry, I misunderstood, but sure, what does a dog's collar have to do with a big business, sorry again."

"It will help us?" they asked in chorus.

I answered yes. I had, of course, no idea what they were asking of me.

CHAPTER SEVENTEEN TWO PAINS AND A MYSTERY

We came out of the Flagellation together. Shlomo and Hanan in hoods and Franciscans from sandals to habit, I, as always, in shirt, pullover, big black shoes with rubber underneath, heavy waterproof canvas jacket. Shlomo even nodded his blessing towards the non-commissioned officer and the soldiers, intent as usual on cleaning their weapons and making coffee. I realized that the patrol had changed but the gestures were still the same. As she said goodbye, Shlomo said, "If a person isn't willing to take some risk for his opinions, either his opinions are worthless, or that person is worthless."
Hanan smiled at me and said: «Father Matteo, you are good».

I saw them move away towards Sant'Anna followed by the non-commissioned officer's distracted gaze. I made my way to the Holy Sepulcher with a question spinning in my head. Why hadn't Hanan and Shlomo told me about Sylvie's kidnapping?

Bishop Lahan was in the paved courtyard in front of the Holy Sepulchre. He nodded to me. He accompanied some students from Beit Sahur University to visit the basilica.
He asked me: "Have you come to tell me something?"
"She didn't tell me the truth."

Bishop Lahan shook his head. There was no truth to tell, but his tone didn't convince me. I was insistent. I spoke about Carlino's collar, about everything that was happening that I didn't understand, and about the fact that he - I was convinced of it - was better informed than me. He smiled and observed how close I had a relationship with the Keeper. I was impatient. If I was going to go on I had to know. I realized, as I said that, that Lahan might as well have spoken back to me, instead, in a low voice, he said, "Hanan was my secretary."

"Has it been or is it still?"

He replied that it was no longer. I told him I had met her and Shlomo and they needed help. She replied, "Hanan knows that to live is to act. Our Lord acted, even on the Cross He acted. Even in death we act. But for Hanan and Shlomo the cross is too heavy».

I asked him what that answer meant. And then I sighed: I was fed up with all those mysteries. He fixed me with an innocent look, so innocent that I asked him point-blank, "Bishop Lahan, what's in Carlino's collar?"

"What the Keeper told you," he replied with a smile and blessed me.

I went to the Keeper. I didn't go anteroom. He offered me a lemonade, he was in a good mood. His legs gave him little pain that day. He explained to me that he was reflecting on Our Lord's childhood to better understand the ways of his preaching about him. At five, he reminded me, children were enrolled in the Casa del Libro, sort of primary school which they attended from dawn to noon six days a week, under the guidance of a teacher. At the age of ten the student moved on to the next level, the House of Wisdom, which lasted three years. Then he continued with other courses to become a rabbi.

«Our Lord's preaching is influenced by the method of the House of Wisdom. Our Lord was tied to the reality in which he lived. And from this comes his attention to man. Attention is the natural religiosity of the spirit. Do you agree with this concept, Father Matteo?»

"The last time we met, Reverend Father, he revealed some things to me, but withheld others."

He rolled his eyes. This time longer, she almost looked for inspiration for a suitable and satisfying answer. She sounded fatherly now.

«Father Matteo, the secret is sometimes like a melody that takes hold of our senses to such an extent that we end up singing it obsessively. It wasn't my intention for this to happen."

I observed that I felt no loss at that tune, but whoever might have heard it out of tune were Shlomo and Hanan. "My dear Shlomo and my dear Hanan, young and naïve!" he exclaimed. I begged him to unfold better.

"We always leave the doors of the possible open," he dismissed me, and this was his explanation.

Saul Bialik's black car was waiting for me in the courtyard of San Salvatore. The usual chauffeur invited me to take a seat in the back seat next to Bialik. I went up automatically, without asking him how he knew I was at the Warden's.

Bialik seemed absorbed, he didn't even greet me: the car took the panoramic view that passes through the buildings of the Hebrew university and descends towards the village of At-Tua. We arrived at the Mount of Olives. We stopped at a checkpoint. Some soldiers were around a car pressed against a wall. Inside, I saw Shlomo and Hanan. Shlomo rested her head on Hanan's shoulder, softly, as if he were talking to her. Tears flooded Bialik's expressionless face. It looked like rain on stone. He said to me in a confident and colder voice than usual, as if commenting on an action that didn't concern him: «Shlomo was driving, he accelerated, the soldiers had to shoot. It's the law. If he had stopped they would have identified them and that was it. They had orders not to touch him or Hanan. It would have been a normal and simple check.

He did something I never imagined. She hugged me for a

long time.

"Father Matteo, is it possible to die like this?"

She sobbed. I realized she didn't want answers. I blessed Shlomo and Hanan. I stopped for a few minutes in prayer. Bialik thanked me and then said in a toneless voice that I had to go to the Keeper. He needed me. Shlomo was a real son to him. As if he had generated it. I looked at the Hebron valley, the nature around and followed the run of a lizard. I thought of Shlomo and Hanan fondly and tenderly. Bialik said to me: "Who will be able to fill the measure of my pain? Who Will it fill the measure of my tears? I suffer because the divine hand took me by the hair before Hanan, Father Matteo». Now she almost screamed.

"I have what I gave!"

He added that he was staying with his boys, just asking me to look after Sylvie. His chauffeur would take me to the Keeper.

I got to San Salvatore in time to see an ambulance in the courtyard, its rear doors still open. Inside, on a litter, the Keeper was lying, his eyes half closed. It seemed to me that he was waving at me. I hurriedly got out of the car. I tried to get closer. Guillermo firmly barred my way. He explained to me that the Keeper could no longer speak. But just before losing consciousness he had expressed a desire to meet me. I told Guillermo that the Guardian had waved at me. Guillermo replied that it was impossible, I had imagined it. I asked him if the Keeper had received word of Shlomo's death. Guillermo rolled his eyes.

"Yes or no?"

I understood that a bitter battle was being fought in Guillermo's soul between silence about every secret concerning his boss and the desire to give me an answer. I decided to help him without compromising his conscience.

"I understand, Guillermo, that he didn't know."

With a sigh of relief he said to me: «Matthew, before losing consciousness, the Reverend Father exclaimed: "The bells are ringing. Yes, it's Palm Sunday. Father Matteo go to the shores of the Sea of Galilee and find the palm trees". I don't know what that means, but perhaps he was already delirious.'

As the ambulance departed I thought back to those words. Only one thing gave me relief: Providence had spared the Keeper the pain of Shlomo's death.

I returned to the Flagellation to reflect. Bialik in those conditions, Shlomo and Hanan dead, the Keeper in the hospital. There was only one person who could help me at this point: the Sheikh. I had to meet him. I called him and Greta, the housekeeper, told me I'd find him at the casino in Jericho. I thought of the night I'd spent with Raed teaching him how to be a dealer. It was just destiny that I set foot in that casino.

Greta sent the car to Allenby bridge where I arrived in a taxi. I got into the Sheikh's car and arrived in Jericho. I entered the casino through a back door. I walked down a narrow corridor, the walls painted red. The floor was covered with an equally red carpet. In front of me, at the end of the corridor, was a small vestibule. A pale man in a white jacket smiled at me welcomingly. He bowed to a stairway leading down to the right, in the direction from which I heard the music.

I found myself in a large room with a high ceiling. Along the dark green walls, at regular intervals, papier-mâché cherubs supported oval mirrors. The spaces between one mirror and another were decorated with stylized drawings painted directly on the wall. In a corner of the room, a bar counter. In the opposite corner the orchestra platform with four musicians who could have been Latin Americans. They wore flashy yellow shirts with puffed sleeves. Next to the orchestra a door closed by a pale green velvet curtain. The rest of the space along the walls was occupied by small booths. Other tables were arranged around the central track.

The little orchestra was playing and two very made-up and rather vulgar girls sketched tango steps on the dance floor with an unconvinced air. The Sheikh was waiting for me at a table in one of the booths.
"It's still early," he explained. "But the atmosphere will soon liven up." A waiter uncorked a bottle of champagne for us.

"Do you have enough money?" the Sheikh asked me. "This crap is going to cost us at least a hundred dollars."

Then he laughed and said not to worry, he offered of course. The same waiter brought various meat and fish dishes and many salads. Without asking me if I was hungry, the Sheikh began to eat. More than eating, he gobbled and moaned.

"Beauty belongs to the youth for whom this earth was created. But it's only a dream. When faced with great pain, I usually react like this. Because I'm partly to blame for what happened." I asked him if he was referring to Shlomo and Hanan by any chance, and in what sense he was guilty. He replied that Shlomo and Hanan trusted him. They were convinced that he would help them. And then he added, "I think I was the last to see them alive."

He explained to me that there was a hotel on the Mount of Olives where he occasionally met his clients. He had to talk to Shlomo and Hanan about a certain matter. Then he had taken a taxi, had passed a checkpoint; Shlomo followed him in his car, he had stopped, but the soldiers had killed him together with Hanan. I replied that Bialik had given me another

version. The Sheikh commented: 'What do you want Bialik to know. He wasn't there. In fact, I'm convinced that he too is a victim. His career is over, his daughter is dead, he no longer has a life.'
"He'd have his granddaughter left, but someone kidnapped her."
"Already. Bialik is alone, without a future and without hope. Then she asked me: "Did Bialik ever talk to you about a perfume?"
"Yup."
"And what did he say to you?"
"That an old friend sends him a bottle every year."
"That old friend is me."
I exclaimed that he was everywhere and knew everyone. He laughed and observed that in the story I was experiencing there were many intrigues, but the skein was unique and I would soon have grasped the thread. I replied that she could also help me. The Sheikh told me that they hadn't spoken to Bialik for years, he only sent him perfume, which was a way to remember Sara. Sara was wonderful, she had always admired her. I asked him how she had known her.
"At the theatre, in New York. She was much better than Saul, and he suffered for it."
"He didn't tell me when he told me about you."
"Probably ashamed of his weakness."
He told me that he had seen Hanan born and considered himself her godfather. By a curious case in his life, which he would later explain to me, he was also linked to Shlomo. He had had the privilege of seeing their love blossom. When Hanan became pregnant with Sylvie, he helped her spend the last few months of her pregnancy away from Bialik. Saul would never have given his consent to marry Shlomo, who held Israeli

citizenship but was not Jewish. I told him that I did not understand this position. He exclaimed: "My poor friends, joy lasts only seven days, while sadness lasts a lifetime!"

It was stronger than me.

"As you can tell you're not a Catholic!"

He gave me a light pinch on the right arm. He exclaimed: «Father Matteo, life would be unbearable if there were no pleasures».

The orchestra had finished playing, the two girls had finished dancing, and one of them met his gaze. They approached the table and smiled. The Sheikh said something. The two girls shrugged and walked away. The Sheikh whispered to me: "I warned them that you are a friar."

I replied that I understood. The Sheikh continued: 'A man's features, that is, the bone structure and the tissue that covers it, are the product of a biological process, but everyone creates his face for himself. He wears it like a mask, a tool to arouse emotions in others that complement his own. If he fears, he will want to be feared, if he desires, he will want to be desired. It is a screen that hides the nakedness of the mind. Only a few painters, Father Matteo, have managed to see the mind through the face.

I was on business in Tunis, among fragrant flowers and courteous gardeners. One day a good friend of mine, the Israeli ambassador, was killed in front of my eyes. A senior PLO official lived in a villa near the hotel where I was staying. One night Mossad agents arrived from the sea and assassinated him.

I went back to my home under Mount Nebo convinced that my fate was bound up with those who killed and those who died, and that peace was my nightmare and my joy, that it was like the bird Rukh which seizes Sindbad and flies with it high into the sky. Sindbad is frightened by Rukh and when Rukh abandons him in a mysterious place he is frightened at first but after some time he is happy. I understood that this was the time of the forest and wild days when everyone followed the strongest.

I had studied an astrological system that applied mathematical rules to the stars. Because the stars, and consequently our lives, follow harmonies and paths that have been set for millennia. There are many variations within each path».

I asked him if he was trying to explain the concept of infinity to me.

«Infinity is marked by the infinite inflections of our imagination, Father Matteo.»

From a small embroidered bag she took a deck of ancient and colorful tarot cards.

«They are the major arcana. Give me four, without turning them over."

I did. She slowly he turned them over and arranged them in a cross, but she didn't read them right away: instead he watched me while I stared at them almost trying to interpret them. She concentrated on silently reading him.

«The Sun above is success, triumph, love. What do you prefer? On the right the Wheel of Fortune is happiness and luck, but on the left is the Devil. And the Devil brings controversy, fatality, and other more unpleasant things."

"What does Death below mean?"

"Take another card."

I caught the Hanged Man. He placed the tarot in the center. He scratched his head and rubbed his forehead. He narrowed his eyes.

"It seems you are close to something very dangerous."
"Pug's collar," I suggested. He shrugged and shook my hand.

"There will be more deaths, I'm afraid," he said seriously. "But she's not in danger, I assure you."
"In Jerusalem you die easily and at all hours."

I realized I had said something trivial and added: «Everywhere people die at all hours and often suddenly, of course, but here death is more unjustified than in other places. Here you die because someone passes by and stabs you without you knowing why. Old Jews die thinking about the Holocaust, young Arabs die thinking about their own Holocaust. It is only death that rules. The Jews have built a state with the idea that it is the last possible border and beyond the border there is only despair and death».
"Do you really think so?"
"Yes, although I wish I didn't think so."

He nodded his head in approval. He ran a hand over his face as if he wanted to dismiss a bad thought. He exclaimed, "I'm a member of this casino! Our slot machine is perfect. A building in good condition, which is a rarity in these parts, a large guarded car park, a five-star hotel. And in front of the hotel, a service station and an open space for the special buses that unload hundreds of customers every night.

The players slip in with a quick step, without thinking that a few hundred meters away there is misery, desperation, refugee camps that date back to 1948. George Habbash began his activity in one of the camps. But just don't imagine what lies beyond the dark and the conscience is saved. Oasis, as this place is called, is worthy of Las Vegas. With an added touch of security. Chandeliers, stained glass windows, halls and a row of metal detectors, just to remind you that we are in

Jericho. You didn't pass the check, but our customers have their data entered into the computer and their face immortalized by a camera hidden behind a fake mirror. Oasis is always full. But you almost don't notice the presence of the players, right?».

I said yes because I understood that he would like it. The Sheikh stretched out his feet. He looked around with evident satisfaction.

"We can talk to those two girls later. Do you like it?"

"Not really," I replied categorically, and shivered as I swallowed a sip of champagne.

He sighed: «Too bad, but we'll have to drink the champagne. It can't be thrown away."

The environment had come alive. The booths were full and more tables had been set up around the dance floor, which soon filled up. It seemed bizarre to me that in those parts Cousins of the Wall and Friends of the Rock danced Latin American rhythms while ignoring each other, but certainly not shooting each other. I smiled to myself as I thought that a concrete possibility of peace was being realized in the casino.

The Sheikh asked me, "What's funny?"

I shook my head and told him. He made a face. Then he laughed too. The air was beginning to be unbreathable, it was hotter and hotter. The Sheikh touched my arm.

"Look," he said.

For a moment a couple dancing in the far corner of the floor blocked my view. Then the couple moved a few centimeters and I saw Giulia Lazzari motionless next to the light green velvet curtain. She wore a grand evening dress, her face was expertly made up. Her hair looked as if it had just come out of the care of a Parisian hairdresser, her mouth was smiling, her bearing proud. Many of her eyes gazed at her with longing and interest.

Giulia Lazzari turned abruptly and headed towards the bar. The Sheikh called a waiter and gave him an order. The man made his way towards the bar where Giulia was drinking, it seemed to me, a coffee. The waiter whispered something to her. Giulia looked our way and for a moment her eyes rested on me without emotion, as if I were any customer. He put down the cup and slowly came towards us. I got up, we hugged. The Sheikh said: «Giulia Lazzari sings here at the casino. She is our attraction. She's extraordinary."

Julia sat down. Me too. I asked her about the baby. The fingers of her right hand moved quickly and grabbed the stem of a goblet. For a moment I feared she was going to break it. On her face in an instant I saw many emotions run: anger, sorrow, pain. Then her fingers left the glass.

"Father Matteo, why didn't you tell me that my husband had been killed?"

I replied a little hesitantly that Ben Gurion Airport hadn't seemed like the right place to reveal it to him. The shadow of a bitter smile appeared on her lips. She was wearily aggressive, as if she had waited for the moment to tell me certain things and now, seeing me confused and embarrassed, she thought it wasn't worth it anymore. She brought her face close to mine and she asked me again: "Why didn't you tell me?"

This time I didn't answer her. I looked at the Sheikh. He watched with affectionate attention, ready to intervene if the confrontation became too bitter.

"You know, before he died my father gave me these words: a person who suffers more than others is worthy of suffering more than others. Father Matteo, I am that person."

He took a long pause. I stiffened and wanted her to keep talking.«Father Matteo, the news of Pascal struck me in

Paris and I felt instantly that the child had died with him. I passed out and when I opened my eyes again in a perfect, white, small hospital room, the baby was no longer in my womb. I went back to my apartment alone, desperate. I lived in an old house on Boulevard Montparnasse with narrow, damp stairs lit by a greenish, almost sepulchral light. In that light, the staircase seemed fantastic, full of mystery and a gloomy silence. One evening as I went up, it seemed to me that a man was crawling along the wall. He wore a pair of dark glasses: when he was in front of me he lifted them and it seemed that he had taken off a mask, so much was the expression on his face changed. His eyelids were ulcerated, he had no eyelashes, and in the midst of that blush two infinitely sad pupils barely opened. In those eyes I saw needles, splinters of wood, pieces of glass, painful thorns. Father Matteo, what pity, what pity! Does he know anything darker than pity?"

I told her that our religion did not consider pity a dark evil, but a joy.

«My pity was unhappy and hopeless, because that face, Father Matteo, was that of Pascal. I had to come back here, find his grave, bury my son next to my husband. And thanks to him,' she pointed to the Sheikh, 'who has always been a good friend of ours, I succeeded. Then he offered me a job. So I sing in the evening and cry during the day."

The Sheikh told me to follow him. Behind the green curtain was an elevator that took us down a dim corridor with numbered doors on either side. Everywhere there was a smell that reminded me of a hospital during visiting hours. The Sheikh opened a door. We entered a large children's playroom. There was Sylvie, who as soon as she saw me she ran towards me, she jumped on my neck and said: «Do you like scrambled eggs?».

I answered yes.

"I eat them here every day. Have you seen how many games I have? Now excuse me, but I have to get back to my computer."

The Sheikh explained to me that it was Giulia who took care of the child. He continued: «Father Matteo, remember, those who are so passionate about life cannot and must not die».

He paused. Then he exclaimed forcefully: «I had never felt so much emotion. Never had I witnessed a higher and more spontaneous miracle of intelligence. Did he understand who I am referring to?"

I shook my head.

«Pascal Aretz, the night he was a guest at Mount Nebo, woke up at dawn and came to see me. You didn't notice it, Father Matteo. Pascal knelt on my bedroom floor. Parallel to him ran a yellow streak of sunlight, straight, very sharp. He told me: "My sobs don't have the power to change reality. But what can we change? Do our tears weigh heavily?". And he concluded: "Every man is an ordinary being to whom anything happens".

Pascal explained to me that he was very worried about the fate of Giulia and their child. I made the mistake of smiling at him. He was still pale, but at that moment all the blood drained from his face, and a dagger appeared in his hand. He stood up and came towards me. I, Father Matteo, know many arts of defense and offense and I didn't want to hurt him too much. I began to circle around him, waiting for the right moment to disarm him. He was clearly beside himself. In hand-to-hand combat, coldness wins. Without him realizing it, I took the dagger from him and locked it in a drawer.

He came to his senses. She asked me to forgive him for that nonsense. He would have confessed his secret to me if I promised to protect Giulia Lazzari and the child. I promised. Pascal sighed for a long time. He hesitated, almost ashamed. Then in one breath he told me that he was terrified of being tortured and that idea was enough to throw him into absolute panic. That was why he had to have Bialik kill him. If the Tsomet agents had used their systems, he would have revealed what they wanted to know. The truth about the Good Soldier, the project of the group they were part of and above all their strategies.»

I asked the Sheikh if he hadn't forgotten something. He looked at me questioning.
"Why did he kidnap Sylvie?"

He laughed for a long time. Then he said: «I could offer you an exchange, Father Matteo. Pug's collar in exchange for Sylvie. But think: it would cause Sylvie more than a problem. True, Sylvie is the Keeper's granddaughter to some extent, but I don't think the Keeper is in a position to comment on that at this time. Now I'm giving you my secret. Nobody gets the money they deserve."

CHAPTER EIGHTEEN THE DEATH OF THE KEEPER AND THE TRUTH OF THE SHEIK

I arrived at the clinic two blocks from the King David with the hope that the Keeper would listen to me. He was hospitalized on the first floor in a room that overlooked an internal garden. The atmosphere seemed calm to me. There was no one at the door. It was ajar, I entered. The Guardian had his eyes closed, his face serene, it seemed to me that he was breathing very slowly. His body was entirely covered by a sheet. Only his right hand was abandoned, parallel to the mattress. I took it gently, touched it with my lips, put it back under the sheet and bowed in deference and affection. I spoke to him thus: «Reverend Father, D'Annunzio writes that it is necessary to kill love for it to revive seven times more ardently. This is exactly what is happening. And you have to help me. We must forget the pain and think that close to us there are only people who have suffered all that can be suffered under heaven. People who also have treasures of tenderness and goodness deep down in their hearts, to be spent without any fear. How many of these people have lost creatures of their own blood?

Reverend Father, you know all the answers. Do you remember what she said to me one of the last times we met? She ordered me to retrieve Carlino's collar. Why is it so important? Would the map with the exact place where the Ark is buried really give the Cousins of the Wall a unique strength, a great political advantage in negotiations with the Friends of the Rock? And the Sacred Nails, which according to Vidigal are hidden in the collar, what value do they have? If they are only a relic, I don't think they can be that decisive. But beyond the Sacred Nails and the Ark, everything that is agitated around the collar seems excessive and false to me. I didn't quite understand what happened. The Sheikh has Sylvie in his custody, who is in a sense his niece. Bialik has only recently learned that Sylvie is Shlomo's daughter. Hanan had kept the name of the child's father from him for years, and Bialik had kept his daughter's secret. Shlomo and Hanan wanted to get married and were killed. But wasn't it easier for them to come and ask for his authoritative intervention against Bialik?

Each moved on its own, and with terrible consequences. I find Giulia Lazzari in Jericho in the Sheikh's casino, who I discover is a friend of Pascal Aretz. Giulia now takes care of Sylvie, whom I met in a room of the casino smiling and happy.

What is the meaning of all this story? And why did you have me elected Discreet? Don't you think I'm just a good archaeologist? Didn't you charge me with too many responsibilities?"

I looked at the Keeper and I didn't understand if he was listening to me. He remained motionless, his body seemed tense in a finished gesture. On the glass of the window overlooking the garden a fly was gliding and its paws irritated me with their noise. A little wind had picked up when I arrived. I had the feeling that the Keeper was trying a cry, the brief twist of a hand. Maybe he was paralysed. It seemed to me that time had stopped. I assumed the Keeper shared my anguish. I whispered a few words to him, sentences. When he got better I'd take him to the American Colony, where we'd sit at an old coffee table with a stained marble top, look at the yellowing pictures on the walls, maybe TE Lawrence, maybe Churchill, maybe Agatha Christie, then we would have had an aperitif, and I would have asked him: "What do you know about the Sheikh, Reverend

Father?"

And he would have replied: "It is you who must tell me about the Sheikh."

I would have told him that I understood why he had sent Sylvester to Cyprus. A sort of exile. In fact, he was aware of the relationship between Sylvester and Shlomo. But he probably didn't know that there was a film documenting them. However, he would have asked me if I had finally understood who the Sheikh was. And I would have replied that the Sheikh worked above all to make money and, having proof of Shlomo's relationship with Silvestro, he had involved me, perhaps so that I would come and tell him about it. For what purpose? That was what I was missing. And he would have stimulated me by saying: «Father Matteo, he is on the right path».

«Yes, of course, the filmed document becomes the subject of negotiation. The Sheikh imagines delivering it, for example, to Bialik."

"In exchange for what, Father Matteo?"

«Of Bialik's renunciation of looking for Carlino's collar. So no one loses face. The Cousins of the Wall are hiding an infamous episode in which one of their officers appears in cahoots with a Franciscan, who in turn is the leader of a gang of young Palestinian terrorists and you, Reverend Father, dismiss a terrible suspicion from the Custody: what the Franciscans are linked to the Intifada."

"It's twisted reasoning, but it could be so."

"Everything is right, Reverend Father."

"Yes, and for this very reason it is good that Carlino's collar remains in our hands."

"The Sheikh wants it."

«But you, Father Matteo, will know how to do the best.»

«Reverend Father, if I look out the window of this room, I see an infinite number of houses and the people who live there. I believe that an extraordinary feeling of peace would take possession of their souls if they understood that the effort of building houses could not have made them selfish. I think the Cousins of the Wall have suffered too much not to understand. We move for men who have suffered great suffering. Men upon whom the ferocity of other men has raged without respite.

A voice behind me exclaimed, "Beautiful words." I whirled around. It was Monsignor Lahan.

"But I've only heard them. The Keeper has been dead for an hour."

The man with the kippah I had seen coming out of the Warden's study entered the room. He introduced himself. It was his cardiologist. He uttered a few cold phrases of circumstance, but I realized that his eyes were shining. Monsignor Lahan wanted to take a walk with me in the garden of the clinic. He said a few words about Shlomo and Hanan.

"My poor friends. Do you know what I told Bialik? Joy lasts only seven days while sadness lasts a lifetime. And he replied that he hates sadness. I observed that he hates all of life then."

I could not find the right words to reply. He continued: "Did you see what a horror in Tiberias? Do you remember when the two Jews from Kibbutz Ginosar found that ancient boat near the shores of the Sea of Galilee? And they said it was Our Lord's boat? It was actually a boat of the time. Now a certain Semadar has set up a vulgar little business. He had two boats identical to the one built by craftsmen who work in the Nile Delta and use a circular saw and wooden nails. The boats cost fifty thousand dollars each, they towed them along the coasts of the Mediterranean, crossed the Galilee in a special convoy and launched them with the names of Peter and Andrew And so the tourists go on a trip on the holy waters remembering Our Lord and the storm.

I looked at him puzzled. I didn't understand. She talked to me about vague things. Then she gave me an open envelope with a letter inside. I recognized the Keeper's handwriting. I read.

«Dear friend and colleague, I entrust you with some free reflections, which continue what we said orally. I know we basically agree. Even if this agreement of ours will have to remain a private dialectical exercise. After all, we represent two Churches and we are not allowed to think differently from our superiors. I fear that Christianity is dying and in its agony it is giving off all kinds of poison. And we, who have the privilege of living where Our Lord was born, are tragic witnesses of his death and experience daily the impossibility of changing history. My feeling is that Judaism will survive. In this tiny territory he offers a monstrous test. Ah, if we had their spiritual strength! In this sense, I wanted to take up with you another theme of our recent conversation. The one on the map that indicates the location of the Ark. The map strengthens Israelis' rights to that land. For these reasons and for those I have described before, it must remain well hidden. She is in safe hands."
I returned the letter to Bishop Lahan.
He asked me, "Is value related to time, in your opinion?"
I told him I had no idea.
«Don't be sad, Father Matteo. Remember, youth is just a slice of madness."

The funeral of the Custos took place privately in his chapel in San Salvatore. The music chosen was the one he loved the most. Mozart's Sonata No. 13 performed by

Glenn Gould. The ceremony was simple and sad. We were all there. Vidigal in the front row had tears in his eyes and was very excited. I took a seat next to him. The mass was celebrated by Guillermo. It seemed right to me: he had spent a part of his life beside the Keeper. Bialik appeared next to me, and he too was very excited. Then I felt a tug on my jacket. It was Sylvie and she was smiling at me. Bialik's eyes widened, she came closer and confidentially shook his hand. Vidigal's funeral homily was concise and moving, and concluded with a sentence that it seemed directed at me: "Fantasy and desire, the Keeper has always said, remain the best weapon for facing reality and the unexpected."

I also saw a person I never imagined could intervene. It was Rabbi Hirsch who told me: «The Custos called me "little man". It was a compliment to me."

To honor the Keeper, I went as promised to the American Colony and sat down at the old coffee table with the slightly stained marble top. I assumed he was there too and ordered the waiter two aperitifs. A familiar voice asked me:

"I can sit down?".

"Of course, you did a good deed."

"I've done so few in my life."

I told the Sheikh that this time he had behaved well. He shrugged and observed, "I was very fond of Shlomo and Hanan. Father Matteo, there are many aspects of the whole story that you don't know yet. I want to help her walk her path."

He ordered a coffee and began to talk.

«As the history books report, on March 24, 1976, a military coup deposed Isabelita Perón from power in Buenos Aires. The government was assumed by a military junta composed of three commanders of the armed forces: Jorge Videla, Emilie Massera and Ramón

Agosti. The history books tell little about those who fight for a cause. They only quote the bosses.

I was a young Peronist. I was arrested one rainy morning on August 20, 1976. At my parents' house. My father disappeared on September 14th, my mother on September 18th. I had a few records left of them, an ice cream maker, a belt and a photo of them dancing the tango. Since then I have had a recurring dream. The doorbell rings. It is my father Rubén. Then I wake up. It's really a dream. Father Matteo, the past exists only for those who have lost it.

Do you know what horror is? Horror is a matter of taste. And I'm not just talking about blood. Imagine my nightmare. I am lying on the torture table, bound with my feet and hands crossed. A young police officer tortures me with a picana, a stick that emits electric shocks, and he asks me where my fellow fighters are hiding. I desperately seek a breather, even a few seconds. I hold my breath and answer: "I don't understand you". Furious, he hits me with another blast and he asks me the question again. "I understand the question, it's you I don't understand." Stay stone. How can it be that a prisoner, in the midst of torture, thinks of posing problems? I'm just looking for a little respite and with my words I found it. He puts the picana down and asks me: "What do you mean?". I answer him: "You are a militant, so am I, but we are on opposite sides. Don't you realize you're doing the dirty work for someone behind a desk? And that when this war is over, they won't need you anymore and they'll dump you?" He stops torturing me and sits next to the grill. "Maybe you're right" he tells me, "but my colleagues and I are getting organised. We will take out these bureaucrats." "You are dumber than I thought" he retorts, "you will end up on this same table."

Enraged, he gives me the last hit of the picana and leaves. I had always thought, even before my kidnapping, that the torturers were human beings like her and like me. I mean that among human beings there are saints and murderers, perverted and normal, a whole range of grays, not just black and white. For me the man who tortured me was not a monster from another planet. He limited himself to carrying out the order received, thus relieving himself of any responsibility. If I had regarded my torturer as a monster, I would have been equal to him, you understand?"

I told him yes. He continued: «From the moment a person was kidnapped, he became a desaparecido. The sequence was: disappearance, torture, death. We spent day and night hooded in a cell called a tube, narrow as it was. We cleaned the latrines, we cooked, and then the picana again Until the transfer came, that is, the execution.

Life was a constant psychological as well as physical torture. We were assigned a code, and from that moment we no longer had to use our name: we had ceased to belong to the world of the living. We couldn't even commit suicide. They were the masters of our lives and we would only die when they decided it.'

The Sheikh was staring at me now. Her eyes were mild and there was a smile on his face.

"Torture degrades victims and perpetrators. It degrades mankind. I, who had always felt like a citizen of the world, found myself lost. Don't you agree with me? Do you know what I was thinking about during the torture? To a train, and I thought that a suitcase looks like a human being because it collects many colored labels on its journey through life. But the labels are only appearances. A facade to present to the world. Only what's inside matters. I thought about this, and after packing my bags I began to think about languages, I wanted to become a citizen of the world, for me all languages were beautiful and I wanted to study them. It was at that point that my condition changed. The breach opened in the balance of my torturer began to bear fruit. He sent a report about me to Massera and the admiral wanted to see me. He told me that he had learned from my torturer – he called him my keeper – that I wanted to be a citizen of the world. It was one of the phrases I often repeated under the picana. He told me that he too, like me, wanted to be a citizen of the world. If only men had been able to live as brothers, and instead there were Communists, Peronists and other wicked people to be eradicated. He made me an offer. If I wanted to become a citizen of the world, I only had to do him one courtesy. To deliver a certain thing to a person. He made me an offer. If I wanted to become a citizen of the world, I only had to do him one courtesy. To deliver a certain thing to a person. He made me an offer. If I wanted to become a citizen of the world, I only had to do him one courtesy. To deliver a certain thing to a person.

They cleaned me of blood and dirt. I had a real meal, then they dressed me up as a military man and put me in a black car. I accomplished the mission. Yes, Father Matteo, it was I who delivered Shlomo in swaddling clothes to the future Custos. Massera kept the pact, I left Argentina.

Do you understand now how responsible I felt for that boy and how now I regret him?

The rest is quite simple. When my work brought me to these parts and I learned who the Keeper was, I went to see him reminding him of our meeting. A sort of complicity arose between us. That's why I recovered that footage in Yemen. It was to save Shlomo, not to blackmail anyone. Is that clear to you now?"

CHAPTER NINETEEN RETURN TO CAPHARNAUM

I left for Capernaum. It was the Sheikh who recommended it to me. More than an advice, he almost tasted like an order, even if he was kind and affectionate. I accepted it as if it were natural that I would go to Galilee to find answers to my questions. He added that my attitude reassured him, he saw me serene and able to face what would certainly have been a complex conclusion. I asked him how much of the truth he already knew and he smiled at me with a hint of bitterness. He nodded his head, rolled his eyes much like the Warden, sighed just as he did, and told me gravely that he still had something to tell me and wanted me to choose freely whether to believe him or not. He then added:

«Remember, Father Matteo, those who understand too much are often unhappy».

While I was driving the car – I had preferred this way to avoid any interlocutor, even a driver –, I went over the last conversation with the Sheikh to decide whether to believe him or not. I kept thinking Shlomo and Hanan had been killed by accident, and he'd replied, 'Anyway, they're gone. Bialik is also a victim. His only daughter is dead and his career is over.'

I told him I still didn't understand. Bialik was no longer deputy director of Tsomet. The Sheikh had explained to me that he had been deposed. He'd had too many failures. First, the deaths of Chephren and Pascal Aretz, killed instead of captured. Chephren, rather than be captured, had allowed himself to drown, and as for Pascal Aretz, I myself had witnessed his end. I replied that it was evident that the two deaths had neither been wanted nor sought by Bialik. The Sheikh had smiled at me. I was a good shepherd of souls but, as far as the logic of the secret services was concerned, I had to learn a lot. I had pointed out to him that I had very little interest in the secret services.

He went on to tell me that, without delving into the methods and systems of the services, Bialik's failures appeared clear. He had objected that, if he had become deputy director of Tsomet, he had certainly had some merit. He replied: «Father Matteo, do you know what gets old quickly? Gratitude".

I had explained to the Sheikh that, as a good shepherd of souls, as he had defined me, I found it grotesque to define two deaths as failures: it really meant not attributing any value to human life. He didn't reply and went on to explain Bialik's third failure, which concerned Carlino's collar. Another story ^ in which his behavior had not met the leaders' expectations. Bialik, contrary to his orders, had disinterested in the collar, worrying only about solving the story of his daughter, the Good Soldier and his niece. I had asked him if the Israelis knew the exact contents of Carlino's collar. The Sheikh spread his arms and replied:
"Everyone has their own idea of the collar. Whatever it contains, it is very important to get hold of it."
"For her too?"

He smiled without answering me. I asked him: "Is Bialik's life in danger?"

"Worse," he replied.

"What could be worse?"

"Take Sylvie away from him, for example. Have him sit for the rest of his years behind a desk and stare at the ceiling."
"But he's already old enough to retire."
"There's never a pension in that trade."

I had asked him if the Keeper was aware of any of this. He answered yes and told me that he and the Keeper moved with the same goals. I replied that, unlike the Keeper, he had never struck me as a holy man. He had said seriously: "Father Matteo, I'm mainly interested in money."

Then he added: «I knew Saul Bialik, but above all I loved Sara, as I have already told you. I was a magician in a Broadway club. I was an attraction, you know?'

Now I understood his skill at playing cards. She had reacted piquedly. Reading tarot cards had no connection with prestidigitation. And she continued: «Sara often came to see me. She admired me. As I admired her. When she entered the stage, the others disappeared. With the blink of an eye she made people laugh or cry, with a wave of her hand she created poetry. I became her best friend and she became my best friend. I know what she's thinking. There was never anything else between us. Because? Maybe because Sara's passion for her threw her all on stage. Maybe because she didn't want to disturb her private order. I could tell you many other things. But feelings of love have unique and inexplicable rhythms. With Bialik relations were correct, nothing more. He seemed like a freak to me. I didn't share, shall we say, her vision of her life. Too much Holocaust in his memory, even if he didn't experience it directly. When Sara died we lost touch. I kept in contact with Hanan, I followed her growth, I met her often. Nothing more with him, but I sent him that perfume every year».

"And he never looked for her?"

"Never, not even when I moved around here."

"Did he know she was here?"

"Of course he knew, though Hanan never told him she was coming to see me." I had observed that Hanan loved secrets: he had even hidden Sylvie's existence from her father.

'Yes,' replied the Sheikh, 'she was like that. Very similar to her wonderful mother. I who have accompanied her growth, who have followed the development of love with Shlomo, who have seen the birth of Sylvie, have not been able to help them. »

I was amazed that he didn't change his tone. Always the same, devoid of emotion. I repeated that I still didn't understand. Shlomo and Hanan had a daughter, but they did not live together and were not married. Bialik had asked me, who moreover was a friar and not a rabbi, to talk to them and see if they were really that united. If I had convinced myself and had convinced him, he would not have opposed the marriage. But why did they need Bialik's permission to get married? Sylvie was five years old. Was it possible that he had been unaware all this time that the child had a father? Even if Hanan hadn't told him anything, how was it possible that he hadn't been suspicious?

The Sheikh had said that my logic was compelling, but I didn't take into account the difficult relationship between father and daughter. Hanan had been very impressed by a phrase her father had once said to her.
"The moment one is no longer a boy, one is dead."

From these words it was possible to understand Bialik's relationship with his daughter. She had to remain a girl and therefore she should never have married. When Bialik first learned of Sylvie's existence, the little girl was two years old. Bialik had considered her a second child, Hanan's younger sister. He was convinced so as not to wonder who his father was. There was no other father but him. Hanan was her Sara and Sylvie a new emanation of Sara, an unexpected and wonderful gift.

"But Bialik couldn't ignore the love between Shlomo and Hanan."

"There was something about him that refused to accept it. Bialik pretended not to know that Shlomo was Hanan's partner. When she told him that they had decided to get married and that Shlomo was Sylvie's father, at first he thought it was a joke in bad taste, for which he didn't understand the reason, then he realized that he was preparing a long nightmare from which it would have been impossible to wake up. His despair was profound. A strong resentment against Shlomo invaded him. He decided that he was ungrateful. Because it was he, Saul Bialik, who had invented an identity for that child without a mother, father or country, responding to the request for help from a Franciscan friend who, before being transferred from Buenos Aires to Jerusalem, had seen deliver, as if it were a package, the newborn. Bialik had chosen a typically Jewish name for the boy, Shlomo, and had made him an Israeli citizen, forging papers. And when his friar friend had been first elected Discreet and then Custos, in agreement with him he had designed a brilliant career for Shlomo in Tsahal. Also because the discreet protection of the Guardian, his good relationship with every Israeli government, right or left, would certainly have helped. And had that ungrateful man like him responded to all the good that had been done to him? By seducing Hanan and forcing a daughter on her. And now he even wanted to force her to marry him. agreeing with him he had designed a brilliant career in Tsahal for Shlomo. Also because the discreet protection of the Guardian, his good relationship with every Israeli government, right or left, would certainly have helped. And had that ungrateful man like him responded to all the good that had been done to him? By seducing Hanan and forcing a daughter on her. And now he even wanted to force her to marry him. agreeing with him he had designed a brilliant career in Tsahal for Shlomo. Also because the discreet protection of the Guardian, his good relationship with every Israeli government, right or left, would certainly have helped. And had that ungrateful man like him responded to all the good that had been done to him? By seducing Hanan and forcing a daughter on her. And now he even wanted to force her to marry him.

But Saul's hell has just opened. Hanan explains to her father what the wedding should be like. The ceremony, which will take place outdoors on the Mount of Olives, will be broadcast live on television. The marriage between a Jewess, daughter of one of the heads of the secret services, with a survivor of the Argentine dictatorship, adopted son of the Custos of the Holy Land, official of the Tsahal thanks to a constructed Israeli citizenship, would have moved the world. Among the guests of honour, the Custos, the Melkite bishop Monsignor Lahan, the most representative rabbis, including Shach and Hirsh, and the Latin, Orthodox and Armenian patriarchs, the Grand Imam of the El Azhar mosque, Sheik Sayed Tantavi, the Grand Mufti and all accredited ambassadors. A testimony of faith, of peace, of love. But Hanan's project doesn't stop there. Another wedding will be celebrated at the same time as him, that of Pascal Aretz, son of Hassan Sueidan Aretz, a Melkite senior leader of the PLO killed in Beirut, with a Jewess of Italian nationality.

Do you understand who I'm talking about? By Giulia Lazzari. Yes, Father Matteo, Giulia's father was a Jew from Ferrara whose name was Levi and who had changed his surname to Lazzari when fascism promulgated the racial laws.

The marriage of those four people would have created an extraordinary precedent and much curiosity in the mighty of the earth. Two couples formed by a Jewess, whose father to escape the horror of the concentration camps had become a Catholic, a Palestinian, whose father had been killed by the Israelis, a Christian who, in order to have an identity and survive the dictatorship who ruled the country in which he was born, had become a Jew, and a Jewess whose only goal was peace with the Palestinians.

Bialik naturally tried to screw up the project. She first told her about the risks to her position, and then concluded that the double marriage would be seen by Israelis as an outrage against the Holocaust. Hanan considered it an old-fashioned and exaggerated speech, he had the feeling that her father wasn't sincere, didn't love her and above all couldn't understand what an extraordinary occasion for peace her double wedding was.

Faced with his daughter's reaction, Bialik was forced to tell her an unpleasant story. The truth about the death of Hassan Sueidan Aretz.

In 1973, during the "Spring of Youth" operation, a commando under the orders of Bialik had landed in Beirut. The goal was to assassinate Arafat's deputy and his right-hand man Hassan Sueidan Aretz, a prominent member of the Melkite community. The two men are killed. The operation goes perfectly, Bialik does not lose a man, and thus begins his brilliant career which will lead him to become number two of Tsomet.

Hanan told everything to Pascal Aretz, and Pascal with great serenity explained to her the purifying meaning of the two marriages. On that occasion, Bialik could have publicly revealed the truth about Hassan Sueidan's death and this would have been a further step on the path to peace. Hanan went back to his father and told him about Pascal's idea. Bialik drove her away. At this point Shlomo, Hanan and Pascal went to see Bishop Lahan, who was fascinated by the project but considered it unfeasible: it was just a wonderful utopia. In their intentions he should have convinced the Grand Mufti and the Grand Imam of El Azhar to attend the wedding. Then Shlomo, Hanan and Pascal went to the Custos and asked him to convince the Armenian, Orthodox and Latin patriarchs, and rabbis Shach and Hirsh.

At this point I would like to go back a bit, to the relationship between Hanan and Giulia. Hanan, who graduated in Architecture in Tel Aviv, goes to Paris. She tells her father that it is a one-year training course. Bialik is proud of his daughter. His dream is that he becomes an architect of international prestige. Actually Hanan is pregnant with Shlomo. During the pregnancy you know Giulia Lazzari. The two women make friends. A strong affinity arises between them: I imagine that Giulia said to Hanan: "I am convinced that the truth is moving and offers every human story the strength to continue".
And I guess Hanan replied: "You are the first angel I meet."

Sylvie was born in Paris. She has two mothers. When Hanan returns to Jerusalem, Sylvie stays with Giulia. Shlomo finds excuses to visit his daughter from time to time. It's easier for Hanan. There are many opportunities. A conference, a seminar. Saul, who has no idea of the truth, is happy that Hanan has taken his profession so seriously. In the meantime Giulia met Pascal Aretz in Paris. When the two couples meet in the French capital, they make plans, they want to carry out some important act: thus the fantasy of the double wedding is born.

Let's go back to the present. When Bialik is informed by Hanan of what she has in mind for her, after having tried in every way to dissuade her, he spreads the rumor that Pascal Aretz is Chefren's deputy. He persuades himself that it can be a winning idea. On the one hand he will regain the trust of the leaders, cracked after the failure in the capture of Khafre, on the other he will undermine Hanan's project.

And we come to you, Father Matteo. His participation is not foreseen. Instead, since the story is a great improviser, she by chance finds herself taking on the role of protagonist. Giulia arrives in Jerusalem to meet Hanan and Shlomo, Bialik intercepts and arrests her. From that moment on, due to that fortuitous meeting with Giulia in Italy, she will become the center of the story.

But Bialik collects a series of errors. He must prevent the double marriage, hand over Pascal to his bosses, take Sylvie. He didn't deal with the story. When she informs him that Giulia is pregnant, Pascal has himself killed to save the child and because he is terrified of torture. Two arguments of those who define themselves as decisive. The idea of marriage between Hanan and Shlomo still stands. The Keeper involves her because she, without knowing it, is already inside the affair. In fact, a Franciscan, Father Silvestro, is allied with Shlomo and helps him go underground. You, Father Matteo, will offer the Custos, who wants to get rid of that dangerous problem, the way to remove it. Duly directed by Muhammad, who is a very knowledgeable policeman, he will discover Sylvester's personal Intifada and report to the Guardian,

I had interrupted the Sheikh by explaining that I hadn't told the Keeper anything. The Sheikh replied that he already knew everything. But he needed a witness. And I turned out to be perfect.

"What does Carlino's collar have to do with all this?"

«Father Matteo, I believe that Carlino's collar was initially a false target. She actually had to find the solution to the real problem, Shlomo and Hanan's marriage. A solution that neither the Keeper, nor Bialik, nor even Lahan had.”

The story was incredible, but for this very reason it could be true. And while he was telling it, I remembered certain things Shlomo and Hanan had said when they came to see me disguised as friars. Hanan had told me, 'My father adores me. His heart is breaking."

And Shlomo had added with a certain coldness: «He's a nice person, I wouldn't want him to suffer too much. I hope he will overcome the problem of our marriage.'

Hanan had replied: “He will never get over it. It's the Russian soul of him. I know that when I get married, he will feel that he has lost everything that made life worth living. I've never met someone as taken with a female figure as my father is with me. I've replaced Mum in all respects, and Sylvie is as if she were his daughter, not her granddaughter. Of course he won't want to hinder my happiness, he's too generous for that.'

As he spoke, I felt a sense of alarm build up in me. Despite the vaguely melodramatic tone, I understood that those sentences made sense.

I had asked the Sheikh: 'You didn't kidnap Sylvie, did you?' He had smiled.

«I see that you begin to understand. Shlomo and Hanan entrusted it to me.”

And after their deaths he had handed Sylvie over to her grandfather, driven by a surge of pity.

There are situations, a playwright once said, that cannot be represented on stage. Situations for which the public can show neither approval nor disapproval, neither sympathy nor antipathy; situations from which no truth, however bitter, can be drawn. Bialik was one of those unhappy beings who cannot distinguish between the vulgarities of real life and the ideal existence of fantasy. When Shlomo and Hanan realized that their lives were worthless, they had been concerned with keeping Sylvie safe. And they had sent her to the Sheikh, who had brought Giulia back from Paris to take care of her.

«Father Matteo, do you want to know where Sylvie is now? Before dying, Bialik gave it to me recommending that I entrust it to Giulia Lazzari. Yes, because he killed himself, in a symbolic place for him: the Mount of Olives, where Hanan and Shlomo wanted to get married and where they died instead. And Sylvie is now in my house on the slopes of Nebo, together with Giulia.»

Perhaps there was some sense in the fact that Bialik had died so tragically, just as he had lived. Special conditions have to be created for the special kind of person that Bialik embodied to exist. I had tried to imagine what they were, without success. I only knew that as long as power had the same strength as law, as long as chaos and anarchy masqueraded as order and truth, despair would prevail in the Holy Land. As the story of Bialik, Shlomo, Hanan, Pascal demonstrated. But those deaths had caused some kind of order. There was a logic that governed everything. Bialik offered Sylvie to Giulia Lazzari in exchange for the life of her child. He actually wanted to save them all. She had a plan in his head. He would offer his bosses a deal in exchange for Carlino's collar and its contents, which he didn't know about but which he assumed was important. Shlomo and Hanan would have gotten married, without that absurd televised ceremony; Sylvie would have grown up attending a Jewish school; Pascal Aretz and Giulia would have been expelled. Events had taken another direction. Besides, Bialik would never have allowed Pascal to undergo harsh interrogation.

"There have been too many misunderstandings in the whole affair and too many things left unsaid," concluded the Sheikh.

"And the candelabra?" I had asked.

"Lahan wanted you to get in touch with me. What better excuse than a sacrilegious theft?"

"Ingenious."

«Now that I've told you what I know – and if you asked me why I'm so well informed, I'd answer that I don't only buy and sell art objects but also news – let's lay the cards on the table.» I had commented that they didn't seem like the right words for a conjurer. And as far as objets d'art were concerned, it seemed to me that he limited himself to buying them.

"I want Carlino's collar, Father Matteo."

"Then you know what's in it."

«Certainly not the map of the Ark of the Covenant nor the Holy Nails. In the Keeper's intention, it was up to her to recover the collar. Let's respect them. Go to Capernaum and ask for Misha Karmi, I can't tell you more."

"Or doesn't want to?"

"I really don't know."

"Why me and not her? I am not convinced by your noble explanation of the Keeper's wishes."

"He'll understand everything when he has the collar in his hand."

Misha Karmi was an Israeli with a lean physique and a healthy appearance who has always lived in contact with nature. He told me that he was fifty-five years old, had three children, four grandchildren, and after spending more than a quarter of a century on a kibbutz, he had decided to change his life. Now, together with a partner, he rented kayaks that adventurous and reckless tourists used to descend the Jordan. His house was located on the shore of the Sea of Galilee, a few hundred yards south of our convent.

He told me it was a wonderful place, a natural park full of palms, rushes, eucalyptus, oaks, and vineyards that gave grapes for nine months of the year. There were birds, foxes, hares, and Kinneret's fish was excellent. I wanted to know if he was a believer.

"I'm a secular Jew who believes in peace," he replied.

It was he who warned me that I was about to meet someone. Misha's house was large and beautiful. I heard barking, Carlino appeared. And behind him was Luca. He was there, right in front of me. I asked him, "Are you real?"

He told me that a spell had protected him. Because he was very ill and had hidden it from everyone except the Keeper. And he added: "How much easier life would be if men were all white or all black and how much easier it would be to behave! In your opinion, Matthew, how many good men love evil and evil men love good? And how can such irreconcilable elements coexist harmoniously in the same hearts?

He didn't wait for my answer. He continued, "Do you know what the curse of the Middle East is? It is the ancient ghost of drought, a drier winter than usual is enough to make it reappear, and here are the half-empty basins, rationing, the specter of war of the water. That ghost is merciless, it's like an image of death carved in an ancient ivory that reaches out its hands towards men, women, children. It has a voracious mouth that hastily swallows lives and dreams. Where we are, those who have water live. Anyone who doesn't have it dies. The Israelis control it, the Palestinians depend on them. Matthew, I've been waiting for you because I'll soon be like a root in a dry land. From pain I will pass to eternal joy».

As he spoke, the sun traced the exact rectangle of the window on the floor, and the shadows of the swallows played with it. It seemed to me that everything was devoid of reality, a simulation of life: even my anguish seemed imaginary.

Luca's pale face, his pure forehead, seemed surrounded by an ashen halo, as he stared at me with an innocent, deep, open gaze. He wore his image of pain as if he were proud of it, as if he wanted to say: I know what it means to suffer. As we embraced, I realized he was dying. He exclaimed: «Look, Matteo, look at my hand, doesn't it seem to you that he has already begun to die? I shall not live much longer and my death must be worthy of my life.'

He whispered to me that the Reverend Father had wanted me to keep Carlino's collar until that moment and that now he would give it to me.

"What's so precious about the collar?" I asked.

"Something only you can understand. The Keeper and I entrust it to you. Always remember that good earth belongs to those who fertilize it, like good books." The last word he uttered, as he handed me the collar, was "peace".

CHAPTER TWENTY TO THE NEBO

To the Custos of the Holy Land, From Ayden melton, Memorial of Moses the Prophet, Mount Nebo, Jordan.

Reverend Father, I think it is my duty, even if I imagine you are in Heaven, to write to tell you the conclusion of this story and to reassure you about the project you had in mind. There have been too many deaths. And for them I hope there is rest.

You can imagine how amazed I was at meeting Luca. And yet, Reverend Father, I should have understood, when you did not attend the funeral and send me, that something was out of tune. The Custos of the Holy Land could not fail to be present at the funeral of the most illustrious Franciscan archaeologist, the one who had discovered the house of the apostle Peter. I didn't get suspicious: she was able to talk to me. Luca, however, was already ill. And she, in agreement with him, had only anticipated his death by some time.

We buried him with Misha in his grave, near Peter's house. What better place? On those stones rested Our Lord and the Apostle Peter. Luca's eternal journey would have been serene, his soul would have carried with it the love that had inspired all his actions. It was only right that his feelings should be honored and the secret of his death respected. I said a prayer with tears in my eyes. Carlino barked for a long time and I remembered another detail that had puzzled me. At Luca's first funeral, Carlino hadn't let out a yelp. Even his escapes now appeared clear to me.

Reverend Father, you once told me that mirrors should wait a moment before reflecting images. If I had thought about it, I would have understood that Carlino's image was confused, imprecise, out of focus. This time, however, Carlino lay down on Luca's grave, without moving away. Misha promised me that she would take care of him. He would not let him lack affection or food.

Reverend Father, some summer evenings as I walked from the Wailing Wall to the Jaffa Gate I thought that our Holy City needed to be saved from violence. You have moved in this direction and I have to conclude your project.

Unfortunately, I understood some things late and I doubt that I have disappointed you. She sent me to Capernaum to Luca's fake funeral to solve Hanan's problems, not to recover Carlino's collar. Luca's supposed death was designed to divert Bialik's attention. Hanan knew that Luca was alive. But he didn't know the existence of the collar. Hanan was in Galilee because she had come to ask Luca, whom she knew, for help with his marriage plan. Bialik had followed her, Tsomet agents were there and had set a trap for a group of guerrillas with avoidable carnage. But there was someone other than Bialik and his bosses who knew of the existence of the collar. The Sheikh, from whom Monsignor Lahan, inspired by you, had sent me to recover the candelabra. In reality, the aim was to put me in touch with those who had tried to protect Pascal Aretz first and then Shlomo. The Sheikh told me that when he began to operate in the Middle East and learned about you, he connected names, years, facts, and proposed an alliance pact. He wanted Pug's collar in exchange for Shlomo's safety. Because? For the Sheikh, the collar would become a source of wealth.

She had to defend the collar, save Shlomo, Hanan, Giulia and Pascal, neutralize Bialik.

The conclusion, Reverend Father is not what you wanted. He could not imagine that there would be so many dead.

As far as my person is concerned, I've wondered for a long time why it involved me. I understood it when I discovered Father Luca's secret.

This really was your masterpiece, Reverend Father, because Pug's collar never existed. That's why the dog had nothing around his neck. Instead, there is an ancient map that Luca always carried with him in an old leather case, and that I was the only one able to decipher, as you and Luca were well aware. She told me about a map, found in Qumram. It was true. What was not true was the content of the map.

It does not report the exact location of the Ark, but the detailed list of water sources in the West Bank. Very ancient sources which, if they still existed, would give those who possess them security and strength. In the hands of the Cousins of the Wall they would stabilize their dominion over the region. In those of the Friends of the Rock they would guarantee their total independence from the Israelis.

I remember what happened when Netaniahu expressed his intention to reduce by sixty per cent the fifty million cubic meters of water that were given annually to Jordan, guaranteed by the peace agreement stipulated in October 1994. The king of Jordan said that Israel was betraying the understandings. Quotas were a Jordanian right, not a concession.

The specter of water warfare is always lurking around here. The tug of war between Israel, Jordan, Syria and the Palestinians for control of the basins between the Yarmuk River, the Jordan, up to the Sea of Galilee and the sources of the West Bank, was not in 1967 one of the causes that unleashed the war of six days? And six years later Assad attacked the Cousins of the Wall by surprise to recapture the headwaters of the Golan Heights and access to the eastern shore of the Sea of Galilee. And what was the real reason that pushed the Turkish government to persecute Öcalan, challenging Italy and half of Europe? The Kurds controlled the most water-rich area of Turkey. It was not possible to make the slightest concession to their demands for independence.

Reverend Father, if the twentieth century was the century of oil, the twenty-first will be that of water.

Whoever owns it becomes its guardian and regulates peace, war and wealth. The guardian of the water, Reverend Father, was you, but the exact location of the sources I could only me to find out. Because it is linked to the mosaics of the church of Santo Stefano in Umm-er-Rasas, my most important archaeological discovery. Twenty-eight images of the city are drawn on the floor of Santo Stefano. Some are identified, some are not. I never understood why. I occasionally indulged in that colorful puzzle. Once I talked about it at length with Luca. And I guess it was Luca himself who connected the unidentified cities with the sources of water. Obviously he talked about it with you. Yes, Reverend Father, I will decipher the drawing of that mosaicist who wanted to deliver the secret of water to his work. But it will take time. That's what I explained to the Sheikh, who asked me to sell each deciphered source to the highest bidder. He says that this way I will have the money to build the roof of the Memorial and to dig wherever I want. For himself he asks for a commission of thirty percent. Of course I said no, but he replied that the word "no" does not exist in his vocabulary.

Tomorrow I will celebrate my sister's wedding. She has finally made up her mind Reverend Father. My whole family is present. Garbo is preparing a Syrian lunch of almond rice, fried chicken, roast. My mother brought from Italy, not trusting the pastry shops in

Amman, the wedding cake with sugar newlyweds firmly planted on top. There are many guests. There is the Sheikh to whom I asked if he would like to do a little penance. He answered yes. He added that he would like to do penance in front of the mosaics of Santo Stefano. I replied that I don't see the slightest problem in pleasing him also because in his eyes they are incomprehensible. A pained grimace appeared on his face.

There is Bishop Lahan who is showing me great friendship and affection. He took care of all the organizational and bureaucratic part of the wedding.

There is Father Silvestro who is a gardener. For some time he will indeed be in penance.

There is Father Vidigal who has decided to write a book about Mary Magdalene, to demonstrate that she was not a redeemed prostitute but a disciple whom Our Lord considered equal to the apostles.

There is Father Guillermo who revealed to me how it was he who entered my studio for the first time, at the beginning of this whole story. He was looking for some notes on the mosaics of Santo Stefano, on the colored enigma, Reverend Father. Evidently Luca had already informed her of my searches, but Guillermo was looking for confirmation. He saw on my desk some sheets with exact reproductions of the mosaics and unidentified cities. This gave her the certainty that I was the right person for his project, so he brought me on board.

I told Father Guillermo that to be forgiven he will need mass as my altar boy. Together with a certain Thompson, an Englishman, who looked for me for a long time to give me an interview. You know, I have little time for such nonsense. First I told him no, then he insisted so much that I made him come to Nebo. He arrived while I was studying a mosaic from the second half of the sixth century: two running animals, which were part of the animated band that decorated the presbytery of Santo Stefano around the altar. He informed me with great impudence that he did not want to talk about the mosaics. He wanted to know my opinion on an Aramaic fragment of the Dead Sea Scrolls, published by his journal. The fragment speaks of the Son of God. An expression which, according to some scholars, does not refer only to Our Lord. According to them, the Son of God would be a tyrant who wages war, but the people of God would have fought and won and finally there would have been peace. A fairy tale. And this Thompson, a sweaty redheaded youth, chased me to Nebo for a fairy tale. Does he know what I did? I told him he had to earn the interview.

Now he's cleaning a mosaic and he seems happy. The work, the effort, are the answer to his questions. It's the best interview I can give him.

A little while ago, Reverend Father, I put my hand under the bed, I took a white, embroidered tablecloth. In front of the kitchen, she can't remember, there is a room almost entirely occupied by a large rectangular table, made of well-seasoned wood. I put the tablecloth on the table, ironed the folds with my hands, made the sign of the cross. From the kitchen, from the other rooms, from outside, the guests arrived, some knelt down, others remained standing. On that table I celebrated mass, I blessed everyone and then I said that we could also celebrate our dinner up there.

"And it won't be the last," laughed Garbo.

The mass was also attended by Moshe Hirsh who followed her smiling, Manfred, an Israeli friend, and Muhammad with his entire family.

Manfred was afraid to bury his mother next to his father at the Mount of Olives cemetery because there is a village of Palestinians there who throw stones on that sacred place. I told Muhammad about it and the village boys stopped throwing stones.

Silvestro came to me and asked me: «Who are you writing to?». I smiled at him without answering him.

He said again: "Now I have to go to the kitchen to cut the salad and clean the potatoes."

A small hand gently squeezed mine.

Sylvie jumped around my neck, kissed me. There was Giulia Lazzari next to her.

"I want to give Sylvie a good education."

I interrupted the letter for a moment. I asked my guests to follow me. I brought them before a ^locked room. I opened the door, we entered. It's a small room, the walls just painted white, there's a table with a few chairs, a single window from which you can see the Jordan, Jericho, Jerusalem. The room smells clean.

"Here," I said, "the pope stopped in prayer. Here, when they want, those who fight in the Holy Land will sign the peace.

We left the room. Silvestro came towards us all happy.

«I dressed the salad with oil and lemon. I hope everyone likes it." Then he sang:

«Matteo, when you need help, come to this friend».

I think I will have to ask a lot for help, but above all from you, Reverend Father, because a few days ago the Chapter elected me Custos. I guess the news won't surprise you. You once said to me: "Our destination has us even if we don't know it yet".

Will we one day be able to offer Jerusalem the peace you had in mind? When I have deciphered the map and the mosaic I will write you another letter, hopefully with an answer.

My most respectful greetings.

Ayden Melton.